Catholic Priests Falsely Accused

The Facts, The Fraud, The Stories

David F. Pierre, Jr.

Mattapoisett, Massachusetts, USA

ISBN-13: 978-1466425330
ISBN-10: 1466425334

Printed in the United States of America.

Cover photograph: "Christ surrounded by angels and saints" (detail), a sixth-century mosaic from Sant'Apollinare Nuovo, in Ravenna, Italy. (iStockphoto)

Contents

Introduction

We must continue to demand justice and compassion for victims of Catholic clergy abuse. This is not optional.

Time and time again in recent years, Catholics and non-Catholics alike have been horrified by the hideous stories of wretched abuse and betrayal committed by men who solemnly vowed to model their lives after Jesus Christ. Disguised as servants of God, these criminal priests devastated countless lives. They pulverized the faith of legions with their revolting and sinful acts.

Throngs of clergy abuse victims have relayed harrowing stories of profound torment. These voices must never be forgotten.

In a pastoral letter in March of 2010, Pope Benedict spoke passionately to the victims of clergy abuse. "I know that nothing can undo the wrong you have endured," said the Holy Father. "Your trust has been betrayed and your dignity has been violated."[1]

In the same letter, Pope Benedict reiterated his call for all bishops "to establish the truth of what happened in the past, to take whatever steps are necessary to prevent it from occurring again, to ensure that the principles of justice are fully respected, and above all, to bring healing to the victims and to all those affected by these egregious crimes."[2]

All people of good will should demand no less.

However, there is a side of this long narrative that is not getting the serious attention it warrants. Countless priests in the United States have been falsely accused of committing horrendous child abuse. Media outlets are all-too-willing to trumpet Catholic clergy misconduct, and they forever proclaim these men as "credibly accused" child molesters.

Within minutes of a single phone call to a diocese, a previously unblemished priest can be removed from ministry and have his name and picture plastered across televisions and newspapers across the country as an "accused child molester." And with the permanence of the Internet, such a brandishing will forever be prominent in the public record. The cleric is defenseless.

The reputation of an upstanding, innocent priest – even one that is long deceased – can be irreparably tarnished with the uncorroborated claim by a lone individual.

Many priests are terrified at just the thought of being falsely accused.

Introduction

The fear of one petrified priest was so overwhelming that a drug addict with a long criminal history successfully extorted $90,000 from the cleric over several months just with the continual threat of filing an abuse accusation against him. (After the innocent priest emptied his personal savings, maxed out his credit cards, and borrowed from friends, he called the police. The fraudster pleaded guilty and was sentenced to 18 months in prison.)[3]

Adding to this issue is the sad fact that priests too often feel unsupported and abandoned by their bishops once they have been accused. The embarrassing past failures of bishops decades ago to properly expel criminal priests have now prompted many leaders to act over-militantly to accusations. Fearing the public criticism that they are "coddling child molesters," bishops seem intent to rid themselves of an accused priest as expeditiously as possible, even if the individual is innocent.

"The attitude of many bishops seems to have changed from an assumption of innocence to a desire to distance oneself as quickly as possible from anyone who is accused," observes Catholic scholar Dr. Jeffrey A. Mirus.[4]

The results for accused priests are feelings of hopelessness, dejection, and bereavement.

"[Priests] feel shunned by their bishops, and describe themselves as lepers," one senior cleric says. "They feel hopeless."[5]

While most accused citizens receive the presumption of being "innocent until proven guilty,"

3

CATHOLIC PRIESTS FALSELY ACCUSED

Catholic priests have not enjoyed this expectation. Rather, the assumption is often the opposite: A priest is immediately suspected as "guilty until proven innocent," if not "guilty until proven *guiltier*," as one lawyer has stated.[6]

Accused innocent priests are allocated the burden of somehow trying to prove they did not do something from decades earlier. How does a guilt-free man go about this?

Nothing can compare to the devastating pain of having been abused as a child. However, as this book explores, the emotional, physical, and ministerial impact of being wrongly denounced as a "credibly accused child molester" is truly monumental. Innocent men, through no fault of their own, have been hurled into a public nightmare.

Take the case of Fr. Daniel J. Maher of the Diocese of Albany (New York). With over four decades of untarnished ministry, a man came forward in 2005 to claim that the priest had raped him on two occasions over thirty years earlier.

Fr. Maher vehemently denied the allegations, yet the diocese promptly removed the priest from ministry and began a thorough investigation. A retired senior detective from the New York State Police interviewed individuals who were reported to have witnessed the crimes, but none of them recalled anything. In other words, the accuser's claim was refuted even by his own witnesses. A diocesan review board concluded that there was "no reasonable cause" to believe the priest commit-ted any wrongdoing at all.[7]

Without any other complaints in his decades-long ministry, Fr. Maher returned to his life as pastor at Ho-ly Cross Church and Holy Cross School. Yet his life was not the same as before.

Even after being exonerated and returned to his parish, the accuser's lawyer and members of an antago-nistic victims-advocacy group called SNAP (Survivors Network of those Abused by Priests) began picketing and leafleting Fr. Maher's parish. Angry protesters greeted Sunday parishioners at Holy Cross Church for several months.

The accuser's lawyer began videotaping parents and students around the church school, and the attor-ney became involved in several confrontations with parishioners. The wild attorney even barged into the church's rectory and school in an effort to videotape Fr. Maher.[8]

While Sunday Mass is supposed to be a time of peaceful worship, for parishioners at Holy Cross Church in Albany, Sunday often became an occasion of dispute and unwanted conflict. During one episode, police ar-rested the local leader of SNAP.[9]

As for the accuser's lawyer, his name was John Aretakis, a shifty man with a lengthy history of being disciplined by the courts of New York. In 2008, after judges had sanctioned the attorney on a number of occa-sions, the State of New York found Aretakis guilty of professional misconduct. It took the extremely rare measure of actually suspending the man's law license for one year. The state cited numerous reasons, including that Aretakis "knowingly made false statements of law and fact," "engaged in undignified and discourteous conduct," and "asserted positions which served to harass and maliciously injure." In 2007, when a judge sanctioned Aretakis, the jurist specifically cited Aretakis' "personal vendetta" against the Catholic Church.[10]

In other words, it is not just the false accusation itself that an innocent priest has to endure. Accused priests often face a multi-pronged attack by a zealous media, earnest lawyers, and wild advocacy groups like SNAP. Ambitious attorneys and SNAP often coach accusers in how to effectively address the media about their claims. Media outlets are more-than-willing to relay accusations, and law enforcement officials are all-too-eager to advance their careers by "taking down" a priest in a high-profile manner.

Many may argue that addressing the topic of falsely accused priests is an attack upon real victims of clergy abuse. This book argues the opposite. One can imagine that there are few greater insults to the devastating pain of actual abuse than someone criminally claiming a stake to this suffering in a fraudulent manner against an innocent man. By forcefully addressing this topic, a more honest, enlightening, and informative perspective is offered in the Catholic Church abuse narrative.

The public deserves that this information be told.

Introduction

NOTES AND REFERENCES

[1] "Pastoral Letter of the Holy Father Pope Benedict XVI to the People of Ireland," March 19, 2010. http://www.vatican.va/holy_father/benedict_xvi/letters/2010/d ocuments/hf_ben-xvi_let_20100319_church-ireland_en.html

[2] Ibid., citing "Address to the Bishops of Ireland," October 28, 2006. http://www.vatican.va/holy_father/benedict_xvi/speeches/2006 /october/documents/hf_ben-xvi_spe_20061028_ad-limina-ireland_en.html

[3] Peter Downs, "Extorting $90,000 from priest earns jail time for Niagara man," *The Standard* (Canada), August 22, 2011.

[4] Dr. Jeff Mirus, "Priestly Vulnerability," August 23, 2011. http://www.catholicculture.org/commentary/otc.cfm?id=849

[5] Austen Ivereigh, "Guilty until proved innocent," *The Tablet* (UK), July 14, 2007. http://www.thetablet.co.uk/article/10060

[6] Telephone interview with Joe Maher, president of Opus Bono Sacerdotii ("Work for the Good of the Priesthood," www.opusbono.org), Tuesday, July 13, 2010. Maher quotes an attorney.

[7] "Father Maher Exonerated of Aretakis Sex Abuse Claim: Long on Accusations and Character Assassinations but Short on Proof and Evidence," *Empire Journal*, September 6, 2005. From http://www.bishop-accountabil-ity.org/news2005_07_12/2005_09_06_EmpireJournal_Father Maher.htm

[8] "Diocese Granted Restraining Order against Aretakis," *Empire Journal*, September 9, 2005. From http://www.bishop-accountability.org/news2005_07_12/2005_09_09_EmpireJournal_Diocese Granted.htm

[9] "SNAP Leader Arrested For Church Protest," *North Country Gazette*, April 9, 2006.
http://www.northcountrygazette.org/articles/040906SNAPArr ested.html

[10] Court document: "In the Matter of John A. Aretakis, an Attorney. Committee on Professional Standards, Petitioner; John A. Aretakis, Respondent. Memorandum and Order," State of New York, Supreme Court, Appellate Division, Third Judicial Department, Decided and Entered: December 11, 2008. D-73-08.

1

A Sampling

In studying the issue of false accusations, one thing becomes clear: There is no "typical" false accusation. Each bogus claim stakes its own unique angle.
Consider these recent cases:

- A 59-year-old man came forward to claim that Fr. Al Gondek, from the Diocese of Charlotte, North Carolina, molested him 47 years earlier while swimming as a 12-year-old at a summer camp in Maryland. It turns out the summer camp did not even exist at the time the man said the abuse occurred. In addition, while administered a polygraph, the innocent Fr. Gondek truthfully stated that he had never even learned how to swim.[1]

- Fr. Thomas White of St. Daniel the Prophet Catholic Church in Wheaton, Illinois, was abruptly removed from ministry after a man filed a lawsuit claiming the priest had sexually abused him 25 years earlier. Yet the accuser's claim "began to fall apart when diocese officials learned of [the man's] criminal background," including multiple guilty pleas for fraud. At first, the accuser claimed that the abuse was a "repressed memory." (More on "repressed memory" in Chapter 9.) But as the walls closed in on his dubious claim, the accuser recanted. A statement filed in county court announced, "[The accuser] herein recants any allegation of sexual or physical contact with Rev. White or any wrongdoing of any kind by Rev. White toward him."[2]

- Few Catholic priests in Louisiana have been more respected than Msgr. Ray Hebert. Yet four men in their late 40's to late 50's came forward to accuse the senior priest of raping and molesting them decades earlier at a Catholic home for troubled teens. One man actually claimed that the priest had brutally raped him more than 20 times.[3] Up until the accusations, the priest's 53-year ministry was without blemish. Finally, nearly *five years* after the original charges, the accusers' lawyers "filed an acknowledgment in court that Msgr. Ray Hebert did not molest their clients." In truth, the veteran priest had barely spent any time in the group home with the boys.

A Sampling

As the head of Associated Catholic Charities, his occasional visits to the home were merely administrative. Defenders of the accusers now claim that the charges were a case of "mistaken identity."[4]

- A man came forward to claim that Fr. Dan Wetzler of Spokane, Washington, had sexually abused him nearly four decades earlier. The man claimed that the priest assaulted him during counseling sessions. The media splashed the name and picture of the previously unblemished priest everywhere. In accordance with the bishops' "zero-tolerance" policy, Fr. Wetzler was ripped from ministry. Finally it was shown that the priest was never even a counselor, as the accuser had claimed. "[Fr. Dan's] name, his whole reputation, has been slandered," concluded a loyal parishioner. "The accusation was bogus from the start," added another. "Father Wetzler is one of the great leaders of the local church." An investigation concluded that "someone else" may have molested the boy.[5]

- An 18-year-old surfaced with the bizarre claim that Fr. Christopher Pliauplis "grabbed his genitals" as they passed each other in the middle of the day in the hallway of a Long Island, New York, high school. Despite the fact that another student and a custodian were in the hallway at the time, and 40 parents were seated in a nearby auditorium, no witnesses could corroborate the claim.[6] Fr. Pliauplis was "devastated" by the accusation as a review board recommended his removal from ministry. In order to defend himself, the priest was forced to fly to the Vatican with his canon lawyer to appeal his removal from the priesthood. After two years, the Vatican finally determined what many had known all along – the event never happened. "They railroaded him," the priest's lawyer explained. "Kids are coming forward and saying falsehoods. The archdiocese is not listening to priests, they're just letting them go."[7]

- With nearly two decades in ministry and no other accusations of impropriety against him, Fr. John Costello, S.J., was abruptly removed from his jobs as a priest and a school teacher in Brighton, New York. A former student materialized to claim that the priest had molested him 24 years earlier. There were months of intense confusion and distress to Fr. Costello, the Jesuit order, and the school community. But then the accuser recanted, claiming that "another priest" had harmed him.[8]

- Bishop Howard Hubbard of the Diocese of Albany has weathered his share of criticism over the years. When the bishop was accused of molestation from decades earlier, the diocesan review board turned to Mary Jo White, a highly respected former federal prosecutor. White and her Manhattan law firm conducted 300 interviews and reviewed more than 20,000 documents. They poured through the bishop's personnel files, phone records, credit card statements, and his personal computer. "One of White's investigators said they even went so far as to look at the types of movies Hubbard rented from a Blockbuster video store."[9] White issued an exhaustively detailed 200-page report, which reportedly cost $2.2 million.[10] It determined there was no evidence at all that the bishop had ever broken his vow of celibacy. The bishop also conclusively passed a lie detector test to affirm that he had never had "sex of any kind" with anyone.[11] "We found nothing," added one of White's investigators.[12] "I feel very embarrassed and very humiliated," said Bishop Hubbard. "But with it all, I really am at peace because I know that I am innocent."[13]

- Fr. Ronald L. Bourgault was another priest who had his name and picture plastered prominently around the Boston media landscape as a "credibly accused" cleric. A man came forward to identify the priest as one who had abused him from over 30 years earlier. The Boston archdiocese quickly suspended the priest. The ravaged Fr. Bourgault was out of ministry for months. The accuser's attorney blasted the archdiocese in the media for its investigation of her client's claim, but then the accuser eventually admitted that he made a "mistake" in identifying Fr. Bourgault. "My client now believes it was not Bourgault who molested him," the man's attorney later acknowledged, in a completely different tone than before.[14]

Such examples, quite sadly, are just the tip of the iceberg. There are countless similar stories that can be told.

NOTES AND REFERENCES

[1] Jill Doss-Raines, "Priest endures 'painful journey'," *The-Dispatch* (NC), December 27, 2007.

[2] Angela Rozas, "Wheaton church gets its priest back," *Chicago Tribune*, March 24, 2004.

[3] Bruce Nolan, "6 Allege Abuse at Catholic Home," *The Times-Picayune* (Louisiana), August 25, 2005. From http://www.bishop-accountability.org/news2005_07_12/2005_08_25_Nolan_6Allege.htm

[4] Bruce Nolan, "Molestation allegations against local Catholic priest withdrawn," *The Times-Picayune* (Louisiana), March 18, 2010.

[5] Virginia de Leon, "Priest Cleared of Abuse: Someone Else Molested Boy in 1960s, Investigation Finds," *Spokane Review* (Washington), February 22, 2003.

A Sampling

[6] Leslie Palma-Simoncek, "Island Priest Removed over Sex Abuse Claim," *Staten Island Advance* (NY), June 22, 2006.

[7] Leslie Palma-Simoncek, "Priest Accused of Molesting Teen Cleared by Vatican," *Staten Island Advance* (NY), June 7, 2008.

[8] Jeffrey Blackwell, "Priest Cleared in Abuse Case," *Democrat and Chronicle*, January 8, 2004.
From http://www.bishop-accountabil-ity.org/news5/2004_01_08_Blackwell_PriestCleared.htm

[9] Michele Morgan Bolton, "Inquiry Clears Hubbard: Albany Ex-prosecutor's examination of bishop's private life finds no proof he broke vow of celibacy," *Times Union*, June 25, 2004.

[10] Fred LeBrun, "A Fair Price for Faith in Hubbard," *Times Union*, August 8, 2004.

[11] Daniel J. Wakin, "Report Clears Bishop in Sexual Misconduct Inquiry," *New York Times*, June 25, 2004.

[12] Bolton, June 25, 2004.

[13] Daniel J. Wakin, "Fighting Claims of Gay Affairs, a Bishop Turns to the Public," *New York Times*, February 18, 2004.

[14] Sacha Pfeiffer, "Cleared priest questions process: Alleged victim ID'd wrong man," *Boston Globe*, February 28, 2003.

2

A Stunning Declaration

In November of 2010, veteran attorney Donald H. Steier submitted what can only be described as a truly stunning declaration to the Los Angeles County Superior Court. With experience with over one hundred investigations into Catholic clergy abuse, the former deputy district attorney of Los Angeles stated that his investigations into claims of sexual abuse by Catholic priests have uncovered vast fraud. His probes, he asserted, have revealed that many accusations being made against Catholic priests are completely false.

In his ten-page missive Mr. Steier relayed, "One retired F.B.I. agent who worked with me to investigate many claims in the Clergy Cases told me, in his opinion, about ONE-HALF of the claims made in the Clergy Cases were either entirely false or so greatly exaggerated that the truth would not have supported a prosecutable claim for childhood sexual abuse" (capital letters are from Mr. Steier).

The counselor also added, "In several cases my investigation has provided objective information that could not be reconciled with the truthfulness of the subjective allegations. In other words, in many cases objective facts showed that accusations were false."

Mr. Steier's declaration was a stunner. Also among his eye-opening statements were the following:

- "I have had accused priest clients take polygraph examinations performed by very experienced former law enforcement experts, including from L.A.P.D. (Los Angeles Police Department), the Sheriff Department, and F.B.I. In many cases the examinations showed my clients' denial of wrongdoing was 'truthful,' and in those cases I offered in writing to the accuser to undergo a similar polygraph examination at my expense. In every case the accuser refused to have his veracity tested by that investigative tool, which is routinely used by intelligence agencies."
- "I am aware of several plaintiffs who testified that they realized that they had been abused only after learning that some other person – sometimes a relative – had received a financial settlement from the Archdiocese or another Catholic institution."
- "In my investigation of many cases, I have seen the stories of some accusers change sig-

nificantly over time, sometimes altering
years, locations, and what activity was alleged – in every case, the changes seemed to
have enabled or enhanced claims against my
clients, or drastically increased alleged damages."

- "I am aware that false memories can also be
  planted or created by various psychological
  processes, including by therapists who might
  be characterized as 'sexual victim advocates,'
  if not outright charlatans."

- "Most of the approximately seven hundred
  psychiatric 'Certificates of Merit' filed in these Clergy Cases, as required by [California
  law], were signed by the same therapist."
  (Note: A "Certificate of Merit" from "a li-
  censed mental health practitioner" is
  required in California before filing a civil
  abuse lawsuit.)

Counselor Steier also took aim at the outspoken,
high-profile, victims advocacy group SNAP (Survivors
Network of those Abused by Priests):

They maintain an interactive Internet website
with a user 'Forum' and 'Message Board,' among
other features, where people can share detailed
information between alleged victims pertaining
to identity of specific alleged perpetrators, their
alleged 'modus operandi,' and other details of alleged molestation. In effect, a person who wanted

to make a false claim of sexual abuse by a priest could go to that website and find a 'blueprint' of factual allegations to make that would coincide with allegations made by other people. Law enforcement also uses the S.N.A.P. website to attempt to locate new victims and allegations against Catholic priests.[1]

Needless to say, SNAP had a fit at the sight of Mr. Steier's declaration. In a frantic press statement following the discovery of the document, SNAP derided the declaration as a "legal maneuver" that was "among the most outrageous and hurtful ever made by a church defense lawyer."[2]

Notably absent from SNAP's objection, however, was any statement noting what Mr. Steier had declared was untrue. Such a glaring omission speaks wonders.

And despite the truly alarming nature of his claims, the secular media completely ignored Mr. Steier's astonishing declaration. Even though Steier's court submission took place practically in its backyard, the *Los Angeles Times* did not report on it at all. (Many secular journalists, including those at the *Los Angeles Times*, the *New York Times*, and the *Boston Globe* were most certainly aware of the document.)

NOTES AND REFERENCES

[1] Images of the court documents of Mr. Steier's declaration can be viewed at TheMediaReport.com, http://www.themediareport.com/jan2011/special-steier-declaration.htm

[2] SNAP press release, December 13, 2010, "Clergy sex abuse victims file complaint against priests' lawyer," at http://www.snapnetwork.org/snap_press_releases/2010_press_releas-es/121310_clergy_sex_abuse_victims_file_complaint_against_priests_lawyer.htm

3

Hard Data

Child welfare advocates and experts in child abuse have long argued that false accusations of child abuse are rare. Historically, this is certainly *true*, and readers must be aware of this.

However, recent data clearly shows that the number of false accusations against Catholic priests has grown dramatically. The news of large monetary settlements, as well as the realization that public disgust about these crimes can be criminally exploited, have resulted in an explosion of fraudulent allegations.

What percentage of accusations against Catholic priests are entirely false or unsubstantiated?

One can start with a range between 17 and 50 percent.

Although major media outlets have nearly universally shied away from this topic, there have been several interesting outputs of information in the last few years that have provided insight into the prevalence of false accusations.

17 percent:

Every year since 2004, Georgetown University's independent Center for Applied Research in the Apostolate (CARA) has released an annual audit report outlining statistics for abuse allegations. No one has seriously challenged the organization's reliability and respectability. In 2011, the annual CARA report revealed that a full 17 percent of the 428 new accusations made in 2010 were completely false or unfounded. This was the highest percentage that the organization recorded since it began tracking such information.[1]

This 17 percent figure can be seen as the *starting point* when determining the prevalence of false accusations. There are scores of accusations that are not deemed false until *years after* the allegations are made. (This book provides several examples. To wit, the 2011 CARA report said there were 25 additional accusations from past years that were found to be false in 2010.[2])

In addition, contrary to the popular perception in the media, dioceses are extremely cautious when determining that an allegation against an accused priest is unfounded or false. Staffed by lay people, many of whom are experts in the field of child abuse, diocesan review boards thoroughly investigate claims to determine their authenticity. (There is *much* more on this in "The truth about diocesan review boards" on page 50.)

25 percent:

In early 2011 this writer had a discussion with a veteran attorney with several years and extensive experience in clergy abuse cases. This lawyer estimated that "one quarter" of the cases were totally false or greatly exaggerated.

("Exaggerated" signifies a situation where an innocent hug or pat on the back is chronicled at the same level of serious sex abuse. Yes, such cases do exist. For example, Rev. Edward Zalewski from the Diocese of Manchester, New Hampshire, is now listed as a "publicly accused" priest on the Internet after a woman actually came forward in 2007 to claim that the cleric "hugged her to his body" in 1956 when she was 12. (That was all.) The priest has had no other allegations against him whatsoever. Fr. Zalewski died in 1976.[3])

32 percent:

This is the most recent and *reliable* figure.

In August 2011, the Archdiocese of Boston made huge headlines when it released a sweeping list of all of its priests who have been publicly accused of abuse in the last several decades. (By the way, despite the fact that dissident groups screamed for years for such a list, when the archdiocese finally did so, they still found reasons to gripe. This just goes to show that some people will *never* be satisfied with *anything* that the Catholic Church does.)

The list included 53 priests who were removed from ministry and/or laicized (removed from the priesthood altogether) after these men were determined to have committed criminal abuse.

Yet the archdiocese also posted a list of 25 priests whose cases were thoroughly investigated and determined to be false ("unsubstantiated" is the word that the archdiocese used.)

With these two numbers, one can arrive at the figure of false accusations being at 32 percent. (Not computed for this figure are the number of dead priests who never had their cases fully investigated (55) and the number of accused priests whose investigations were still in progress (22) at the time of the list being released.)[4]

45 percent:

In 2006, years before the Archdiocese of Boston released its lists, veteran writer Gail Besse exclusively reported data from the area. Of 71 complaints filed against Boston-area priests just for the period of July 2003 to December 2005, the archdiocesan review board determined that there was not any probable cause of abuse in 32 of those cases (which equals 45 percent).[5]

This high figure for this particular time period may be explained by the fact that in 2003 there was enormous publicity when the Archdiocese of Boston paid out tens of millions of dollars to hundreds of individuals claiming abuse by priests. Most cases were never even fully investigated, and many later turned out to be false. Yet even accusers with false claims were allowed to retain their sizable settlements.

50 percent:

As relayed in Chapter 2, according to a sworn declaration submitted to the Los Angeles County Superior Court in November of 2010, attorney Donald Steier claimed, "One retired F.B.I. agent who worked with me to investigate many claims in the Clergy Cases told me, in his opinion, about ONE-HALF of the claims made in the Clergy Cases were either entirely false [or] greatly exaggerated" (capital letters in the original).[6]

In seeking to determine the truth about claims against priests, lawyers and diocesan officials have aggressively utilized expert crime investigators. The claims by veteran investigators must be seriously considered. Most often, these detectives are professionals with decades of fact-finding experience. These seasoned individuals approach their tasks seriously with the goal of getting to the veracity of the issue at hand.

With these various sources of data, it is not unreasonable for an observer to deduce that approximately *one third* of all abuse accusations against Catholic priests are entirely false or greatly exaggerated.

Again – it must be noted: Whether the figure is 25 percent, 32 percent, or 50 percent, the egregious and abominable harm committed by criminal priests must never be forgotten. These figures cannot distract us from the utmost necessity to recognize genuine victims of abuse and the obligation to demand justice and compassion.

CATHOLIC PRIESTS FALSELY ACCUSED

[NOTE: This is another contentious issue with which the advocacy group SNAP has tried to mislead the public. SNAP has continued to cite a 2002 *New York Times* article that purported to claim that the Honorable Patrick J. Schiltz, a highly respected jurist with extensive experience in clergy abuse cases, said there were "fewer than ten" false claims in "over 500 cases" with which he dealt.[7]

For SNAP to continue to cite this article as a source for false accusations is incredibly dishonest for several reasons:

1. The article, from 2002, dates before the giant outbreak of high-profile, large monetary settlements with the Catholic Church.

2. Judge Schiltz has said that his 500-plus cases did not just involve the Catholic Church, but "every Christian denomination."[8]

3. Most importantly, most of the cases which the jurist handled did not even involve the sexual abuse of a minor, which is the real issue at hand.

In 2003, Judge Schiltz wrote:

> In the 500-plus cases on which I worked, pastors were accused of a breathtaking array of misconduct. By far, the most common allegation was that the pastor had engaged in a sexual relationship with an adult congregant – a relationship that appeared to be consensual but was alleged to be abusive because of the disparity in power between the pastor and the congregant. Other common allegations were that the pastor had verbally propositioned the plaintiff, exposed him-

self to her, used sexual language that made her feel uncomfortable, induced her to reveal details of her sexual history, brushed up against her, kissed her on the mouth, delivered 'lingering hugs,' or bought her flowers. In one case in which I was not involved, 'an unsolicited kiss and a rub on the back' resulted in a thirteen-count complaint, several years of litigation, and, among other things, a forty-five page federal district court opinion.[9]

The bottom line: the *New York Times* and SNAP clearly have mischaracterized Judge Schiltz and misrepresented the prevalence of false accusations.]

NOTES AND REFERENCES

[1] Center for Applied Research in the Apostolate, "2010 Annual Report on the Implementation of the Charter for the Protection of Children and Young People," March 2011, page 40. http://www.bishop-accountability.org/usccb/implementation/report_on_2010.pdf

[2] Ibid., page 40.

[3] See the entry at http://bishop-accountability.org/priestdb/PriestDBbylastName-Z.html

[4] All lists of accused priests can be found at the web site of the Archdiocese of Boston, http://www.bostoncatholic.org/Offices-And-Services/Office-Detail.aspx?id=21314&pid=21606

[5] Gail Besse, "Ousted priest wages battle to clear name, return to ministry," *National Catholic Register*, May 5, 2006.

[6] Images of the court documents of Mr. Steier's declaration can be viewed at TheMediaReport.com, http://www.themediareport.com/jan2011/special-steier-declaration.htm

[7] The *New York Times* article is, Sam Dillon, "Doubt Is Cast On Accuser Of 2 Priests, Judge Says," *New York Times*, August 31, 2002.

[8] Patrick J. Schiltz, "The Impact of Clergy Sexual Misconduct Litigation on Religious Liberty," *Boston College Law Review*, 44 B.C.L. Rev. 949 (2003) (Vol. 4, Issue 4, 2003).

[9] Ibid.

4

Father Roger Jacques, Archdiocese of Boston

"Father Roger was – as a pastor, as a priest, as a human being – an outstanding and remarkable man," says a woman who was a longtime and faithful parishioner at St. Joseph Church in Waltham, Massachusetts.

"He brought to the church tremendous warmth and reality. His presence among the people was a very kind, listening presence. He was a very human fellow who participated with everyone and had a very pleasant time with everyone as well. He was a great priest."

"And to have this thing happen to him, and the manner with which it was done, was just overwhelming," says the woman.

"This thing" began on a Sunday afternoon in October 2002 in a working-class suburb of Boston. Fr.

Roger N. Jacques had been serving as pastor at St. Joseph for seven years.

During a friendly ministerial gathering in a hall underneath the church, Fr. Jacques was called away to take a telephone call.

Upon taking the call, an Archdiocese of Boston official informed him that a woman had made a complaint of sexual abuse against him dating back two decades when he served in another parish.

"There has to be some mistake," said Fr. Jacques.

"There is not," the official curtly replied.

Fr. Jacques was stunned.

The parishioner recalls the moment that Fr. Roger returned to the church hall after receiving the devastating phone call.

"As he came in, he was different man than when he left," the witness says. "I looked at him and asked, 'What happened?'

"I was overwhelmed," the woman adds. "I couldn't even think. It was unbelievable."

Fr. Jacques and parishioners were bewildered and upset, but there was little time for discussion.

The official had told Fr. Jacques that he had a mere 24 hours to gather his belongings and report to the chancery office in Boston.

The life of Fr. Roger Jacques would never be the same.

After arriving at the chancery office, Fr. Jacques joined in a meeting with the same archdiocesan official with whom he had spoken on the phone. A note-taker was also present. Curiously, the session began with a prayer for the alleged victim.

"He had obviously already drawn his own conclusion as to who the victim was. I found the prayer to be totally insensitive to me," Fr. Roger says. "I sat in silence as the official prayed for someone who had falsely accused me of some kind of sexual impropriety. Why wasn't he praying for the truth?"

The official peppered him with questions, but the answers that Fr. Jacques gave were irrelevant. The next move had already been pre-determined.

Even with no other allegations against him in over two decades in ministry, the archdiocese immediately removed him from his parish, and Fr. Jacques was forbidden to perform duties as a priest.

The next day, the *Boston Globe* and other media outlets gladly trumpeted the story of another Catholic priest "credibly accused of sexual misconduct with a minor." Fr. Jacques was tossed in to the heap as one of "those pedophile priests."

Missing from the tsunami of media coverage, however, was the fact that the accuser's claims embodied several hallmarks of a false accusation. In claiming she was molested at age 10 or 11 in the early 1980's, the woman's charges had several glaring problems and inconsistencies.

For example, the accuser claimed to have "recalled" her alleged abuse only after a therapist administered so-called "hypnosis therapy" upon her in 1998. (Meanwhile, the psychological community has thoroughly discredited hypnosis therapy, and it has completely debunked the theory of "repressed memory." (See Chapter 9.))

In addition, the woman did not come forward publicly with her allegation until October 2002, near the height of the media attention over the clergy scandals.

Another problem was a radical change that the woman made in her complaint against the pastor. She originally complained in October 2002 that Fr. Jacques had lain in bed with her on top of her covers. Yet a few months later, in the following year, her civil complaint was amended to state that the priest's behavior included "raping" her. The woman also added the claim that *another* priest had molested her as well, around age 6. (An investigation exonerated this other man also.)

Meanwhile, the accuser declined three invitations over a number of months to substantiate her allegations under oath.

The inconsistencies and oddities were glaring, and it is startling to think that such a flimsy accusation could wreck the livelihood of a previously unblemished priest.

The pastor fought vociferously and insistently to have his case adjudicated, so he could be cleared and returned to ministry, yet the process was frustratingly slow and difficult.

"Everything was an impossibility," recalls Fr. Roger. "Even with my attorney, it was an uphill battle, just to get information. Rather than being innocent until proven guilty, it felt like you had been proven guilty, and now you had to prove your innocence."

In the meantime, a rabid media widely cited Fr. Jacques as "an accused pedophile priest."

Meanwhile, the false accusation was taking a terrible toll on Fr. Roger's family, especially his aging mother, Marianne.

Fr. Roger went to his mother the day after the accusation in the hope that she would get the news directly from him rather than from the media. Not surprisingly, Fr. Roger's news startled her.

"I would say her reaction was quiet astonishment," says the priest. "Though I tried to spend some time with her, it was almost as if she had gone into shock."

Time passed, and Marianne Jacques was hospitalized in 2004.

"I went to my canonical attorney," remembers the priest. "I asked, 'Is there something we can do to move this process along? This is taking forever. I would like for this thing to be resolved in the event that something should happen to my mother, at least give her the peace of mind that her son is not a sexual molester.'"

Sadly, it was not to be. As Fr. Roger continued to labor to have his name cleared, Marianne Jacques suddenly passed away in January 2005.

Those who knew Marianne Jacques have said that the false accusation against her son took a wicked toll on her.

"I can remember Roger's mother reading things in the newspaper," says a family friend, "and I am convinced that her death was caused earlier by this kind of experience with her son. I really believe this woman died earlier than she would have."

As Fr. Jacques grieved with his siblings and other family members, he had to seek permission from the archdiocese to preside at his own mother's funeral. Fortunately, his request was approved.

"I am grateful that my mother and father instilled faith in me when I was a toddler," says Fr. Jacques. "I could not have possibly gotten through such a desolate period of time without the gift of faith for support."

In April 2006, the day that Fr. Roger had waited years to arrive finally came. Following a thorough investigation of the claims against Fr. Jacques, a Boston archdiocesan tribunal of canonical judges unanimously determined that the allegation against him was completely unsubstantiated. The Congregation of the Doctrine of the Faith at the Vatican agreed, and in December 2006, over four years after the original accusation, the archdiocese was able to announce that it was reinstating Fr. Jacques.

Many may think that an exoneration puts an end to a simple "unfortunate" episode in a priest's life. Sadly, nothing can be further from the truth.

In addition to the crushing professional and personal impact, there is often a tremendous financial burden.

In the case of Fr. Jacques, the spiritual leader of a thriving suburban church had been reduced to delivering newspapers just to have basic necessities.

Father Roger Jacques

Most notably, legal fees mounted rapidly. In the four years it took Father Jacques to clear his name, the pastor amassed legal costs totaling $33,000.

Throughout Fr. Jacques' ordeal, communication with the archdiocese was an incredible frustration. Letters to the archdiocese went unanswered, or the priest would wait months for a response. Sadly, it is a complaint that is all too common among accused priests.

As Fr. Roger desperately sought to clear his name and return to ministry, an event transpired that made this goal even more difficult than he could have imagined.

In October of 2003, only a year after the accusation against Fr. Jacques surfaced, the Archdiocese of Boston agreed to an $85 million settlement with 552 people who claimed to have been abused by priests.

As a result of this landmark agreement, Fr. Jacques' accuser likely collected between $80,000 and $300,000.

This was money paid to a woman whose accusations were later determined to be false. Even after Fr. Jacques was exonerated, the archdiocese made no effort to recoup any of the money that it had given to her.

As Fr. Roger witnessed the woman who lodged a false accusation against him receive a sizable settlement, he was tens of thousands in debt.

How was the accuser able to score her settlement?

CATHOLIC PRIESTS FALSELY ACCUSED

Amidst the media frenzy of 2002 and 2003, an avalanche of claims inundated the Archdiocese of Boston. They involved hundreds of individuals against hundreds of priests, many of whom were deceased.

Angry victims, advocacy groups, lawyers, and media folks demanded that these accusers be given compensation. It would have been impossible for the Church to litigate all of the claims in a court of law. It simply could not happen. There were simply too many claims involving too many priests over different periods of time. And too many people were demanding compensatory justice.

The archdiocese had no choice but to enter into a large-scale "blanket" settlement to compensate all of the claimants.

As a result, nearly all accusers were able to collect a settlement, regardless of the merits of the various claims.

Although the archdiocese did not admit guilt in the cases it settled, it surely led to the public perception that all of the accused priests were indeed guilty.

[In my previous book, *Double Standard*, I relayed how a similar scenario occurred in Los Angeles. In 2006 and 2007, the Archdiocese of Los Angeles paid out $720 million to about 550 individuals. A number of accusers collected sizable settlements even though their claims were found to be completely false and/or unsubstantiated.]

After Fr. Jacques was exonerated in 2006, a leading Boston charity group reviewed the priest's case. It determined that the Archdiocese of Boston should reimburse the priest for all of his legal costs. Yet when the time came to pay up, the diocese initially paid Fr. Jacques only $20,000, still leaving him $13,000 in the red. It was only until July 2011, nearly *nine years* after the original accusation, that the remaining amount was paid in full and that Fr. Roger could say he was debt free from lawyer's fees.

"This allegation took nine years out of my life. And those were nine years where it was like being under house arrest," says Fr. Jacques.

In studying Fr. Jacques' case, one glaring question beckons: Why did it take so long to exonerate a priest who was so obviously innocent?

One answer may lie in the timing of the accusation. The month of October 2002, in which the woman first accused Fr. Jacques, continued to yield a never-ending tsunami of media coverage of the scandals. The *Boston Globe*, for example, was profiling the Catholic Church abuse scandals at a rate of nearly *three news items per day*. Following the *Globe*'s lead, other local news outlets followed with their own rabid coverage. While many cases were all-too-atrocious and true, it got to the point that one could not turn to any media at all without being reminded of the "Catholic Church abuse crisis."

It seems that the Church was simply ill-equipped to properly handle the deluge of claims. In the craze of media coverage, innocent men like Fr. Roger Jacques were trashed in the process. In early 2003, the Archdiocese of Boston admitted that it was up against a difficult "logjam" of cases that it had to administer.

"Our legal system is set up so that you are innocent until proven guilty," says Fr. Roger. "But the crazy [2002] frenzy changed that. Once you were accused, it was assumed that you were guilty."

Trial by obituary

Bishop Juan Arzube died in Los Angeles on Christmas Day 2007. When he was installed as a bishop in 1971, he was one of only a few Hispanic bishops in the United States. Arzube was quite popular for the work he did with the Spanish-speaking communities in Los Angeles, and the bishop spearheaded several organizations to serve them.

When the *Los Angeles Times* finally got around to publishing his obituary nearly three weeks after his death, here is the photo that accompanied the article:

Los Angeles Times

ACCUSED
Juan Arzube denied molestation charges, but his case was included in the archdiocese's $660-million settlement last July.

That's right. The paper stamped the word "ACCUSED" under the man's picture *in his obituary*. Although Bishop Arzube retired in 1993 and had been in frail health since 2002 (he lived in a nursing house), a single individual came forward in 2003 to accuse Bishop

Arzube of abuse back in the mid-1970's. (2003 was the year in which a California bill lifted the statute of limitations and allowed anyone to come forward with any accusation, no matter how long ago.[1])

The *Times* entitled the obituary, "L.A. bishop was lauded as an activist but tainted by accusation," and devoted nearly 30 percent of the article to the single allegation. The obituary quoted generously from the accuser's attorney and allowed him to present the case against Arzube for his anonymous client.[2]

Arzube vehemently denied the accusation against him, and he even demanded to meet with his accuser. (He did.) As with nearly all of the cases brought forward in 2002 and 2003, there was never a trial or hearing of any kind on this case. And because of the "blanket settlement" that the archdiocese arranged with victims' lawyers and insurance companies in July of 2007, the accuser received a sizable award from the record $660 million agreement.

There were never any other accusations against Bishop Arzube.

This single, uncorroborated accusation was enough for the *Los Angeles Times* to soil the man's obituary.

Father Roger Jacques

NOTES AND REFERENCES

[1] I chronicle this troubling California legislation in my previous book, *Double Standard*.

[2] Mary Rourke, "L.A. bishop was lauded as an activist but tainted by accusation," *Los Angeles Times*, January 12, 2008.

5

Father Robert Poandl, Glenmary Home Missioners

According to the accuser of Fr. Robert F. Poandl, the abuse by the Glenmary order priest so "ruined his life," it affected a promising football career. The accuser reportedly said that he had been courted by a number of Division I schools for his gridiron prowess.

There was one problem, however. The boy did not even play football beyond his sophomore year in high school. For the times that he did play, his contributions were hardly noteworthy.

"If somebody lies about something like that, it's got to mean something," one of Father Poandl's lawyers said, stating the obvious.[1]

In January of 2010, a grand jury in West Virginia indicted Fr. Poandl on frightening charges of 1st degree sexual assault, 1st degree sexual abuse, and sexual abuse by a custodian for an incident that allegedly took place nearly two decades earlier, in the early 1990's.[2]

Yet as the case moved forward, it became apparent that the credibility of the accuser was seriously problematic.

When Fr. Poandl's defense requested the accuser's medical records, the accuser took them into his own hands. According to the presiding judge, he then deliberately removed several items.[3] Not only was this action possibly criminal, a number of those medical records may have contained information that could have exonerated the accused priest.[4]

Angered at the gross attempt to manipulate the judicial system and deceive the court, the judge for the case determined that the accuser completely "manipulated the process."

The presiding judge was so convinced of the dishonesty of the accuser that he executed the rare motion of dismissing the case against Fr. Poandl "with prejudice," meaning that state prosecutors could not charge the priest with the same crime again.[5]

In his order dismissing the case, the judge really let the accuser have it:

> It seems to the Court that one who has strong feeling regarding the circumstances as he has alleged them to occur, to the point of saying that this crime "ruined his life" and that he was contemplating both suicide and homicide, would be

obliged and eager to be forthright in order to get the truth the Court seeks. In this case, he has fallen well short of that obligation.

Following the ruling, Fr. Poandl's attorney declared to the *Charleston Gazette* that, with the exception of some adoption cases she had handled, the case was the most satisfying result in 30 years of practicing law.[6]

"From the beginning it was clear to me that this man was innocent," attorney Anita H. Ashley said.[7]

In over 40 years in ministry, Fr. Poandl had never been accused of any other impropriety before.

"Of course, I had known that this man was not trustworthy from the moment that he accused me," said the innocent priest. "I knew that I had not hurt him in any way, let alone committed that terrible crime against him. I also know that such lying makes it all the harder for any true victim of such a crime to come forth and be believed. But until [the court ruling], it was simply my word against [his] – and because of some very sad history in our Church, my word was strongly questioned."[8]

The accuser proved himself to be completely untrustworthy, which should not have been surprising, because as the case had moved closer to trial, the claims against the priest began to disintegrate.

According to the accuser, Fr. Poandl asked the 10-year-old's mother in the early 1990's if she would allow the boy to accompany him on a trip from Cincinnati to a West Virginia parish. Poandl reportedly wanted the boy to join him on the trip "to talk to him to keep him awake."[9]

However, the original complaint from the accuser was that Fr. Poandl committed his crime in 1992 in a city called Beckley, West Virginia. By the time the case was about to go to trial, the charge was that the crime occurred in 1991 in a place called Spencer, over two hours away.[10]

Fr. Poandl's attorneys presented evidence that not only did he not take anyone with him on his trip to West Virginia, but that he did not even leave for his trip from Cincinnati to begin with. In addition, he did not return to Cincinnati after leaving Spencer, where he stopped for only a few hours. Meanwhile, a detailed diary kept by a nun secretary at the Spencer church disproved the accuser's claim, showing that Paondl was alone for his stay.

"The kid made the whole thing up," said another one of the priest's attorneys.

"The judge concluded (the accuser) is not credible," the lawyer continued. "You can't trust him. They were trying to manipulate the evidence to convict an innocent man. Only a person without a conscience would do something like that."[11]

In another startling chapter to this episode, the advocacy group SNAP continued to publicly side with the discredited accuser. Even after the accuser had shown himself to be completely untrustworthy, and even after Fr. Poandl was exonerated, Judy Jones, the clumsy "Midwest Director" of SNAP, actually characterized the accuser as "very credible and caring."[12]

SNAP remained steadfast in its attack on Fr. Poandl and the Church. SNAP's national director, the wobbly David Clohessy, attacked the priest for "exploiting a legal technicality." He then charged Church officials of "violating their pledges" to "put the safety of kids first [and] keep credibly accused priests out of parishes."[13]

One cannot help wonder about the integrity of a group that asserts that attempting to deceive the court is merely a "legal technicality."

The <u>truth</u> about diocesan review boards/abuse panels

In 2002, the bishops in the United States approved the Charter for the Protection of Children and Young People.

Article Two of the charter mandated that every diocese establish a review board to manage accusations of abuse that come to its attention. (Review boards are often referred to in the media as "abuse panels.")

The charter requires that a majority of a panel be composed of lay people who are not Church employees.

Several dioceses have taken the additional measure of filling their panels with individuals who are experts in child sexual abuse. It is quite common for these panels to consist of child welfare advocates, social workers, therapists, child psychologists, mental health experts, and health care professionals. Many panels are also represented with individuals who were actual victims of Catholic clergy abuse.

In other words, these diocesan review boards are very often composed of individuals who have profound sympathy for victims of abuse. They seek to protect children and get to the truth about abuse claims that are brought to their attention. Contrary to the portrait that claims are shoddily handled, these boards often take exceptional care to thoroughly investigate abuse accusations.

Yet media folks and litigation attorneys would have you believe that these panels consist of twelve priests sitting around a table callously conspiring of ways to exonerate their child-molesting friends. Nothing could be further from the truth.

Aggressive lawyers have mocked these diocesan abuse boards as "kangaroo courts" when a group finds that a client's accusation is bogus or unfounded. (These same lawyers are silent, however, when a panel affirms an allegation, which is *more often* the case.)

The time has come for the truth to be told about diocesan abuse panels. The Catholic Church is determined to rid itself of the "filth" of sexual abuse, and these panels have been a very effective tool in its effort to do so.

NOTES AND REFERENCES

[1] David Hedges, "Judge Tosses Sex Abuse Case Against Priest," *Times Record*, September 2, 2010. From http://www.bishop-accountabil-ity.org/news2010/09_10/2010_09_02_Hedges_JudgeTosses.htm

[2] Carrie Whitaker, "Priest in Local Order Faces Abuse Charges," *Cincinnati Enquirer*, February 2, 2010.

[3] Hedges, September 2, 2010.

[4] "Judge dismisses 'with prejudice' sex abuse charges against Catholic priest," Catholic News Agency, September 2, 2010. From http://www.catholicnewsagency.com/news/judge-dismisses-with-prejudice-sex-abuse-charges-against-catholic-priest/

[5] Catholic News Agency, September 2, 2010.

[6] Andrew Clevenger, "Roane Judge Dismisses Priest's 1991 Molestation Charges," *Charleston Gazette*, August 30, 2010.

[7] Ibid.

[8] Ibid.

[9] Hedges, September 2, 2010.

[10] Ibid.

[11] Ibid.

[12] SNAP press release, August 30, 2010, "Trial vs. accused predator priest dismissed; SNAP responds," at http://www.snapnetwork.org/snap_statements/2010_statements/083010_trial_vs_accused_predator_priest_dismissed_snap_responds.htm

[13] SNAP press release, September 14, 2010, "Accused predator priest put back in parish," at http://www.snapnetwork.org/snap_press_releases/2010_press_releases/091410_accused_predator_priest_put_back_in_parish.htm

6

Msgr. William McCarthy, Diocese of Paterson, NJ

The ordeal of Monsignor William McCarthy is yet another hallmark example of a case that never should have lasted as long as it did. The fact that this ordeal removed a beloved pastor from ministry *for five years* is truly astounding.

Like so many other cases, the ordeal of Msgr. McCarthy bears all the hallmarks of injustice: a bizarre accusation, unscrupulous police work, rampant unfairness, and poor judgment.

With nearly four decades into ministry, Msgr. McCarthy had never received any complaints of impropriety whatsoever. Yet on February 3, 2003, a police detective abruptly arrived at Msgr. McCarthy's office at St. Rose of Lima Church in East Hanover, New Jersey, with a stunning announcement: "You have been accused of molesting two little sisters, Nora and Mary, in 1980."

Msgr. McCarthy was shocked. "Surely the detective will go back and discover he is chasing after a lead that is based on false information," he thought.

Unfortunately, the Irish-born priest's contemplation was simply wishful thinking. Over the course of the next several weeks, the combative detective aggressively investigated Msgr. McCarthy. He administered a dubious and possibly rigged lie-detector test, after which the investigator abruptly claimed, "You failed, and you are guilty." (The monsignor later conclusively passed a test from an independent source.) The tenacious detective then aggressively tried to get the senior priest to sign to a confession.

"I will not sign my name to a lie," the priest responded. "Never."

Where did the 23-year-old allegation of abuse by Msgr. McCarthy come from?

For starters, it did not come from the alleged victims or the girls' parents. The source of the false charge was a pair of vindictive women with an old grudge against the priest. The women felt that the priest had undeservedly received part of a family inheritance.

When the detective first approached the grown women to inform them that Msgr. McCarthy had molested them over twenty years earlier, the women denied that any such thing happened.

Yet the detective persisted.

"You don't remember because it was so painful and you buried it, but he did molest you," maintained the insistent investigator to the girls. (The detective was trying to propose the debunked and discredited theory of "repressed memory" on the girls. (See Chapter 9.))

The mother of the girls also denied that the pastor had ever done anything inappropriate with his young daughters. She reportedly said, "He never molested my girls, for if he had done so, I would have killed him."

As is often the case with false accusations, the nature of the charges against Msgr. McCarthy changed over time. The original accusation was that the priest molested the girls *once* during a single visit to their home. As time passed it was asserted that he had gone to the girls' home *seven* times and had molested them with the aid of hand puppets. (Yes, hand puppets.) The girls' ages at which these alleged events happened also changed.

With a clear presentation of the facts, any clear-thinking observer would have concluded that the charges against Msgr. McCarthy were completely unfounded. The accusation originated from a third party; the alleged victims denied any molestation; and the mother of the alleged victims refuted the charges. Case closed? Unfortunately not.

The case against Msgr. McCarthy surfaced in the months following the 2002 Dallas Charter from the United States Conference of Catholic Bishops. Although it was not the intention of the bishops at the time, the prelates' efforts to aggressively combat criminal molesting priests resulted in a warped atmosphere of "guilty until proven innocent."

Lest they be accused of "harboring child molesters" or "coddling pedophiles" by activist groups and the media, bishops often began to take aggressive and swift measures to try to make accused priests simply "go away."

Such was the case with Msgr. McCarthy. In a shocking effort to bypass Church law and proper protocol, the monsignor's superior sent a letter to the Vatican requesting the *immediate laicization* of the senior priest. "Father McCarthy committed an egregious act," claimed the bishop. "He was molesting two young sisters."

Fortunately, the Vatican did not agree to the bishop's request. If there is a hero in Msgr. McCarthy's narrative, it would be Cardinal Joseph Ratzinger (now Pope Benedict XVI), who insisted that canon law be followed and that a canonical trial be held. (New Jersey Bishop Arthur J. Serratelli, the bishop who replaced the one who originally removed and attempted to laicize Msgr. McCarthy, also deserves special notice for his compassion and understanding to the pastor's ordeal.)

It is a good thing that the canonical trial took place, because it proved to be the liberating measure.

By the time the trial took place in January 2007, which was *four years* after the original accusation, even the nefarious police detective knew that the case against the monsignor was corrupt. In addition, all civil charges against Msgr. McCarthy were dropped years earlier.

During the week-long ecclesiastical trial, the judges forcefully questioned Msgr. McCarthy along with several civil and church witnesses. It was the moment of truth for the senior priest.

Finally, in September 2007, Msgr. McCarthy's canon lawyer called to inform the waiting pastor that the panel of judges had unanimously exonerated him.

"I am vindicated," Msgr. McCarthy told the New Jersey *Star-Ledger*.[1]

Msgr. McCarthy's ordeal was not without some sobering lessons, however. He has chronicled his stunning account in an astonishing book, *The Conspiracy: An Innocent Priest* (iUniverse, 2010).

The senior priest experienced a grim lesson in the American justice system. He witnessed how the desire for professional victories often trumps honesty and truth in the world of law enforcement. Msgr. McCarthy saw that a conviction or a confession from a Catholic priest would be viewed as a boon for the career of a successful detective. "A feather in his cap or another notch in his gun handle," the priest observed.

The intense desire to "nab a priest" often leads to dubious police tactics, which Msgr. McCarthy experienced first-hand.

> "I am told that in the process of getting a suspect to sign a confession of guilt, he is regularly given a fake like detector test, all 'legal,' and then the suspect is then told that he lied in denying he had committed the crime. Then all kinds of mental manipulation is applied on the suspect for hours upon hours ...

"The interrogator is trained to ignore normal rules of decent behavior ...

"When I finally read [the detective's] report, which was not given to my canon lawyer until a year [after the accusation], I did not recognize a word of the actual dialogue that took place behind closed doors. [The detective] had 'made up' a horrific story designed to shock and outrage anyone who read it, especially the prosecutor and my bishop ..."

Msgr. McCarthy now realizes that he should have acted much differently following the accusation from law enforcement.

"If I had chosen silence from the moment that detective first accused me, and referred him to my lawyer, I would not be in the position I am in today. As my lawyer, Gerry Rooney, told me, 'Priests are too trusting.' At first I thought the detective was being my friend, and he had my best interests at heart; when in fact he was my deadly enemy. He was only interested in ultimately getting me to sign a confession. I knew I was innocent, thus believed I had nothing to fear, and only wanted to clear my name. I naively felt I could just sit down with the detective and convince him that I was totally innocent. I now realize he had a whole hidden agenda ...

"Even if they have done nothing wrong, priests should get an attorney, and remain quiet – which also means not talking to reporters. It's too easy for words to get twisted."

Unfortunately, Msgr. McCarthy's assessment of the Church's handling of his case is not much better.

"Falsely accused priests want to believe their bishops will protect them ... but too often Church officials have their own agendas. They are busy protecting themselves against possible civil suits. It is not in the dioceses' best interests to believe a priest is innocent because the allegation carries so much weight in society. Thus, [bishops] generally believe the best course of action in all instances is to presume guilt first and sort out the facts later."

Msgr. McCarthy believes that a more just system would involve a screening and an investigation of an allegation before accusations are made public.

"Because of the rise in false allegations, the accused should be afforded anonymity until a determination or admission can be obtained."[2]

Msgr. McCarthy has provided a very valuable first-hand perspective of a false accusation.

NOTES AND REFERENCES

1 Bill Swayze, "Vatican clears East Hanover priest of sex abuse charges," *The Star-Ledger* (New Jersey), May 2, 2008.

2 All quotations from this chapter, unless otherwise noted, are from Monsignor William McCarthy's book: Monsignor William McCarthy, *The Conspiracy: An Innocent Priest* (Bloomington, Minn.: iUniverse.com), 2010. The author is grateful to Monsignor McCarthy for his kind permission to allow quoting from his fine book.

7

Fr. Charles Murphy, Archdiocese of Boston

The very popular and beloved Rev. Charles Murphy of the Archdiocese of Boston was not only the victim of one, but two, totally bogus abuse accusations. As is the case with so many other priests, the ordeal of Fr. Murphy illustrates the brutal harm that false accusations can inflict on one's ministry and wellbeing.

The accusations against Fr. Murphy were so egregiously false that the *Boston Globe*, a newspaper that rarely misses an opportunity to browbeat the Catholic Church (and has barely touched the topic of false accusations), took the rare measure of profiling the priest's heart-wrenching ordeals.

In a moving tribute to the man following his death, the *Globe*'s Brian McGrory described the crushing emotional and physical toll that the devastating episodes had on the man and his priesthood.

When Fr. Murphy died at age 77 on June 11, 2011, he did not suffer from any tangible malady. McGrory explained:

> They brought Murphy to a hospice [] a couple of weeks ago after doctors determined there was nothing left to be done. There was no cancer, no apparent physical disease, just a broken 77-year-old heart that refused to mend.[1]

In other words, it was the overwhelming agony of the false accusations that deteriorated Fr. Murphy. The two fraudulent claims obliterated the spirit of the beloved pastor, who joyfully lived for ministering to prisoners and assisting the deaf.

"Fr. Charlie," as he was known to those around him, was hearing impaired, although that did not hinder him a bit in enjoying his favorite free-time activity, ice hockey. The energetic priest coached and played hockey in the American Hearing Impaired Hockey Association even into his seventies.[2]

"He was a wonderful man," said a long-time co-worker. "He was the epitome of what a priest should be. He had a great sense of humor and was always available to his parishioners. He had a dry Irish wit that we always appreciated, and he was such a nice man."[3]

"He told me [ ] that he never stopped praying for anybody," one of Fr. Murphy's parishioners remembered. "He was such a good man who spent his life in the service of God. He was a wonderful and faithful servant and he was so loved. He could laugh and he had a twinkle in his eye."[4]

"He was a wonderful priest, prayerful and dedicated to the mission of Jesus," said a fellow priest and close friend of Fr. Murphy. "He was truly a good shepherd. The burden of the heavy cross of two false accusations became his mission right to the end, until the Lord Jesus lifted it from his back and welcomed him home."

Although Fr. Murphy appeared to fully bounce back after the first accusation, it was the second removal that emotionally devastated him. As the second charge surfaced, Fr. Murphy had to cancel a long-planned party to celebrate his *50th anniversary* as a priest. The emotional desolation led the once-happy pastor to antidepression medication.[5]

Family members and those around Fr. Murphy witnessed the annihilating impact that the second false charge imposed on him.

"It seems like he died of a broken heart, if such a thing is possible," said a former priest who worked with the popular pastor.[6]

"I can't believe what he went through," said one of the priest's parishioners. "He was absolutely hurt by it all. The second time he was accused, I think it crushed him."[7]

The first false charge against Fr. Charlie was filed in 2004 by woman claiming abuse decades earlier as a young girl. She eventually withdrew her claim a couple of years later.

"It was a nightmare for him," said veteran Boston attorney Timothy P. O'Neill, who represented the Rev. Murphy. "There was no credibility (in the charges) whatsoever."[8]

The second bogus accusation came from a man with major financial problems, which included owing mounds of child support. He also had a history of deceit to the point that even those in his family could not trust him.

In fact, the family of the second accuser was embarrassed and ashamed for the fraud that the young man committed against the innocent priest. Such was this shame that the father of the accuser actually appeared at Fr. Murphy's funeral to apologize to the priest's family.

"He apologized to me for what his son did," said Kevin Murphy, one of Fr. Charlie's brothers. "The father felt that it was his fault for not raising his son right. He wished that he could have stopped his son from what he was doing, because Father Murphy did not deserve this."

Yet the criminal individuals who lodged the phony charges were not the only villains in these episodes.

The other brute in Fr. Murphy's ordeal was high-profile victim attorney Mitchell Garabedian, who has lined his pockets with millions of dollars from suing the Catholic Church, mostly in the Boston area. It was Garabedian who widely trumpeted the fraudulent charges against the innocent Fr. Murphy even though the accusations had no merit whatsoever. (It was also

Garabedian who was the attorney who represented the accuser of Fr. Jacques, profiled in Chapter 4.)

Over the previous decade, it was the *Boston Globe* that was instrumental in building Garabedian's clout, public profile, and bank account during the paper's never-ending coverage of the Catholic Church scandals. The *Globe* showered Garabedian with the kind of glowing coverage that most lawyers can only dream of.

Therefore, in the paper's moving tribute to Fr. Charlie Murphy, it was somewhat astonishing to see *Globe* reporter McGrory criticize Garabedian for his handling of the accusations against the innocent priest:

"What he did was a disgrace."[9]

A disgrace, indeed.

NOTES AND REFERENCES

[1] Brian McGrory, "Collateral damage," *Boston Globe*, June 15, 2011.

[2] Ed Baker, "Weymouth church faithful eulogize Rev. Murphy," *Weymouth News*, June 20, 2011.

[3] Ibid.

[4] Ibid.

[5] McGrory, June 15, 2011.

6 Baker, June 20, 2011.

7 Ibid.

8 Dennis Tatz, "Priest Cleared of Abuse Charges: the Rev. Murphy Will Return to St. Francis Xavier Church in Weymouth," *The Patriot Ledger* (Mass.), April 12, 2006.

9 McGrory, June 15, 2011.

Cardinal Roger Mahony, Archdiocese of Los Angeles

"May you rot in hell you pile of crap!"

"Let's tar and feather this ped-pleaser and run him out of town."

"I hope that this protector of child predators ROTS IN HELL like he so rightly deserves. Its (sic) anybody's guess how many children he may have also sexually preyed upon."[1]

Those are readers of the *Los Angeles Times* posting comments about Cardinal Roger M. Mahony upon his exit as archbishop of Los Angeles in February 2011.

What many of those readers may not have known is that Cardinal Mahony was not just the subject of one false abuse accusation, but two of them.

In the first accusation, a 51-year-old mentally ill woman came forward in April 2002 to accuse the cardinal of abusing her. She relayed a vague and bizarre episode which she said had happened decades earlier when she was a student at San Joaquin Memorial High School in Fresno, California.

"I know it doesn't make sense," the woman said. "I can't even tell you when it happened. But I passed out one day near the band room, and when I woke up my pants were off and then I saw Mahony's face. And then I passed out again."[2]

Then the woman told the *Fresno Bee* that she did not even know if she was even molested or touched by then-Monsignor Mahony.

"I was unconscious. I don't know if [Cardinal Mahony] molested me, but he could have," the woman said.[3]

Uh-huh.

As journalists further questioned the woman about her claim, it became increasingly clear that the woman was quite unstable. She openly admitted that she was diagnosed with schizophrenia in the early 1970's. She also acknowledged that she came forward with her claim in large part because the state was about to cut her disability payments and she desperately needed some cash.

In addition, the *Los Angeles Times* reported, "[The accuser] also said that nearly everyone she has encountered in her life – from her parents and other family members to her high school classmates to her former co-workers – have either molested, abused or emotionally mistreated her."[4]

The police thoroughly investigated the woman's claim and cleared the cardinal.

Then, a few months later, a "con artist with a criminal history of fraud, theft and impersonating a police officer" came forward to claim that the cardinal had molested him in 1982 when the cleric served as a bishop in Stockton.[5]

This second accusation was so egregiously false that law officials actually decided to criminally charge the man with an attempt to extort the Catholic Church.

The *Los Angeles Times* quoted a California county prosecutor. "I'm very pleased that we were able to apprehend this suspect," said District Attorney John D. Phillips. "There are legitimate victims of this type of crime, and this makes it more difficult and burdensome for people that may have a legitimate case."[6]

One cannot help but wonder if the cardinal's high public profile facilitated and expedited the confirmation of his innocence. As soon as the media scrutinized the nature of the allegations, it was obvious to any clear-thinking person that the accusations were ridiculous.

In this case, it appears that the high-public profile of Cardinal Mahony worked to his advantage in facilitating the establishment of his innocence. Journalists were more eager to take the time and explore the veracity of the claims against him. Under close exami-

CATHOLIC PRIESTS FALSELY ACCUSED

nation, one could clearly see that the accusations against him were false.

But what about the typical parish priest with almost no public media profile at all? The media rarely scrutinizes accusations against regular parish priests in the same critical manner with which those against Cardinal Mahony were. (Recall also the high-profile 1993 accusation against Chicago's Joseph Cardinal Bernardin. The "victim" gave a lengthy and tearful account of his "abuse" on CNN and received huge media coverage. The media ran wild with the story until the accuser essentially recanted his claim and admitted that his memory was "not reliable." He also dropped a $10 million lawsuit.)

One cannot help but think that if the media scrutinized the abuse claims against regular parish priests at the same level as a cardinal, more fraudulent accusations would be exposed.

NOTES AND REFERENCES

[1] The Times has archived the article, and the comments are no longer viewable, but the piece is, Mitchell Landsberg, "Roger Mahony leaves a mixed legacy," *Los Angeles Times*, February 23, 2011.

[2] Mark Arax and Larry Stammer, "Mahony's accuser describes history of mental problems," *Los Angeles Times*, April 7, 2002.

[3] David R. Price, Ph.D., and James J. McDonald, Jr., "The Problem of False Claims of Clergy Sexual Abuse," *Risk Management*, January 2003.

[4] Arax and Stammer, April 2002.

[5] Andrew Blankstein, "Mahoney accuser held in Stockton," *Los Angeles Times*, September 5, 2002.

[6] Ibid.

9

Categories of
False Accusations

False accusations take many different forms.
There is no way a book can chronicle all of the various
structures of untruthful claims. Yet here are five general categories into which many false accusations fall:

1. The "repressed memory" accusation:
Many individuals have come forward publicly to
claim that a priest molested them years earlier (and often decades earlier) after asserting that they
"repressed" the memory of the abuse having occurred.

According to the psychological theory of "repressed memory," the intense trauma of abuse causes
an individual to completely forget that it happened. The
person is simply unable to recall it. Then, usually
through the suggestive questioning of an unprincipled

therapist, often under "hypnosis," this person eventually "recalls" the crime as happening.

Unfortunately, the media have been woefully uncritical when reporting cases in which an individual invokes "repressed memory" when claiming abuse by a priest from decades earlier.

Although this theory may *sound* legitimate, in reality it is not.

Dr. Richard J. McNally is the Director of Clinical Training in the Department of Psychology at Harvard University. As one of the world's leading experts in the field of memory, he has 250 publications to his credit, including the heralded 2003 book, *Remembering Trauma*.

In a 2005 letter to the California Supreme Court, which was handling a case in which "repressed memory" was debated, Dr. McNally asserted:

> "The notion that traumatic events can be repressed and later recovered is the most pernicious bit of folklore ever to infect psychology and psychiatry. It has provided the theoretical basis for 'recovered memory therapy' – the worst catastrophe to befall the mental health field since the lobotomy era."[1]

Many other prominent experts agree. "Repressed memory" is simply bogus.

Dr. Grant Devilly, from the Psychological Health research unit at Griffith University, agrees with Dr. McNally. Devilly says that memories of terrifying experiences work in the *opposite* manner of repressed memory theory. People rather wish they could forget their traumatic experiences.

"It's the opposite. They wish they couldn't think about it," says Devilly.[2]

Then there is Dr. James McGaugh from the University of California, Irvine. His expertise in the area of memory was once profiled on CBS' *60 Minutes* program. Regarding the issue of "repressed memory," Dr. McGaugh said in a 2010 book,

> "I do not believe there's such a thing as repressed memory. I haven't seen a single instance in which a memory was completely repressed and popped up again.
> "I go on science, not fads. And there's absolutely no proof that it can happen. Zero. None. Niente. Nada. All my research says that strong emotional experiences leave emotionally strong memories. Being sexually molested would certainly qualify."[3]

Indeed, this is an issue that must be approached with caution and sensitivity. Not all clergy abuse victims invoke "repressed memory." The memory of actual awful abuse is all too real and devastating.

"Repressed memory" should not be confused with instances in which an abused individual minimizes the awful harm that was done and comes to the harsh realization later in life of having been abused. Indeed, as Harvard's Dr. McNally has explained, many victims only come to the understanding of the damage done to them years later after reassessing their hideous experiences. There can be intense suffering when victims reexamine their childhood abuse later in life.[4]

"Seeing the event through the eyes of an adult, they realize what has happened to them and now they experience the emotional turmoil of trauma," says Dr. McNally. The trauma is equivalent to post-traumatic stress disorder (PTSD). Fortunately, therapy under the direction of a competent psychologist has been shown to be very helpful to victims of PTSD.

"Things have changed, happily. We now have treatments that work," adds Dr. McNally.[5]

One final note: It is important to know that in the rare moments that "repressed memory" is challenged in the media, victim advocates will vehemently and vocally complain to writers and editors who dare to challenge the bogus theory. Such attackers will falsely claim that there is a legitimate "other side" to this issue. There isn't. The public should be very aware of this.

To repeat the words of Dr. McNally, "repressed memory therapy" is indeed "the worst catastrophe to befall the mental health field since the lobotomy era."

2. The "dead priest" accusation:

This one is pretty self-explanatory. Dead people can't defend themselves.

"Respect the dead"? Sadly, this dictum does not apply to Catholic priests.

The high number of abuse accusations against priests who are already deceased may shock many readers.

Categories of False Accusations

According to the Center for Applied Research in the Apostolate (CARA), the Georgetown University-based research group that carefully audits Catholic clergy abuse each year, over 43% of all priests who were accused of abuse in 2010 were deceased.[6] This figure has almost gone unreported in the media.

Indeed, in August 2011, when the Archdiocese of Boston released its catalog of 195 priests who had been publicly accused of abuse over the past decades, a full 43% of the men had already died.[7]

How can a dead person be defended?

In July of 2010, Archbishop Charles Chaput of Denver released a press statement exonerating Monsignor William Higgins of a single charge of abuse against him. Msgr. Higgins died in 1967 after over five decades as a priest. He had never faced any complaint of abuse whatsoever until *42 years after his death*, when a lone woman came forward in 2009 with a charge.[8]

As Vincent Carroll at *The Denver Post* later reported, the woman's story was rife with inconsistencies and evasiveness. Even the accuser's lawyer was found to have contacted the woman's therapist in an attempt to manipulate a timeline – an action that essentially amounted to evidence tampering.

The extreme length of time that had passed since the alleged incidents actually made the case somewhat bizarre. The accuser finally dismissed her case, after which the *Post*'s Carroll spoke to the archdiocese's attorney.

"Higgins was born in 1890 and died in 1967," the lawyer said. "And so I find myself defending a case where both the alleged wrongful conduct and the priest's death occurred before I was even born."[9]

It is a sad truth that many accusations are filed against priests who are already deceased. Meanwhile, the accusers of these dead priests are still often able to collect sizable monetary settlements for their claims.

In the Archdiocese of Los Angeles alone, for example, a full 30% of accused priests were dead at the time of the accusations made against them, yet the accusers of these priests still received a significant share of $720 million from two arrangements in 2006 and 2007.[10]

3. The "me too" accusation:

In the "me too" accusation, a deceitful individual comes forward to fraudulently accuse a priest that is already notorious as an awful abuser. Usually the priest's history has already been well publicized in the media. Oftentimes, the priest is deceased or incarcerated.

If the deceitful individual can prove that he or she was a member at a parish where a notorious priest was located, the person often has a solid case with little else to prove. The abusive record of the priest has already been firmly established. Unless a diocese can find an egregious problem with the claim (e.g., the accuser did not even live in the town or attend the parish where the priest resided), a diocese often has little choice but to accept such a claim.

4. Simple criminal fraud

It is a sad fact of human nature that unscrupulous and criminal minds will even exploit the atrocious crime of child abuse in order to obtain monetary profit.

When people pick up a newspaper and read about individuals being rewarded hundreds of thousands of dollars in claims that were never even investigated, it is an unfortunate truth that some will manipulate this situation in an effort to get in on the action.

As noted above, between 2006 and 2007, the Archdiocese of Los Angeles paid out $720 million in two "blanket" settlements to about 550 individuals claiming abuse back to 1930. (Yes, that's an average of *over $1 million* per claimant.) Nearly all of these individuals had only come forward in recent years. Although a number of the claims were all-too-devastating and true, very few were actually investigated for their veracity. Even in cases in which the claims were later found to be false, plaintiffs still retained their sizable settlements. (I wrote about such episodes in Los Angeles in my previous book, *Double Standard*.)

With the aid of an eager media and unscrupulous lawyers, it is not hard to imagine how fraudulent people will try to nefariously obtain a settlement.

As early as 2001, a Boston lawyer wrote, "I have some contacts in the prison system, having been an attorney for some time, and it has been made known to me that [accusing a Catholic priest of abuse] is a current and popular scam."[11]

A year later, in 2002, the Diocese of Manchester, New Hampshire, faced accusations of abuse from 62 individuals. Rather than spending the time and resources looking into the merits of the accusations, "Diocesan officials did not even ask for specifics such as the dates and specific allegations for the claims," New Hampshire's *Union Leader* reported.[12]

"Some victims made claims in the past month, and because of the timing of negotiations, gained closure in just a matter of days," reported the Nashua *Telegraph* (N.H.)[13]

"I've never seen anything like it," a pleased, and much richer, plaintiff attorney admitted.[14]

When sizable money is handed out in large-scale, blanket settlements without any thorough examinations, it is not hard to imagine that corrupt individuals will seize upon their own opportunities.

And as this book illustrates, these blanket settlements also make it more difficult for priests and bishops to later declare any innocence after large amounts of cash have already been doled out.

5. Psychological illness:

This one is a sensitive issue, yet it appears that a sizable number of people who file false accusations may suffer from mental illness.

A January 2003 article for a business periodical theorized that "more likely" "a false claim could be the result of a psychological illness."[15]

The article chronicled a number of psychological conditions, including displacement, factitious disorder, personality disorder, autistic fantasy, and projective identification, that could be foundations for an adult to falsely accuse a Catholic priest of childhood abuse.

Adding to this issue is the undeniable fact that advocacy groups and lawyers often coach accusers how to most effectively present their claims to the public.

For many years now, David Clohessy, the national director of SNAP, has been orchestrating a workshop at the organization's annual conference. The goal of the presentation is to instruct accusers how to publicly showcase their charges. The presentation promises to deliver "practical 'how-to's'" as well as "skills that will help get journalists' attention."[16]

In August 2011, a report from the Catholic League revealed exactly what some of these "how-to's" and "skills" entail. For one, Clohessy instructs accusers to hold press conferences outside chancery offices and police stations. This provides a much-appreciated and desirable visual element for the media to utilize. It also makes it easier for journalists to follow up on the accusation with Church or law officials if they wish to.

Among the other tips from Clohessy that the Catholic League uncovered:

- Accusers should "display holy childhood photos!" SNAP believes this advice is so important that it adds, "If you don't have compelling holy childhood photos, we can provide you with photos of other kids that can be held up for the cameras."

- Accusers should use "feeling words" in interviews: "I was scared. I was suicidal." Be sad and not mad. The goal is to make an emotional connection with the audience.
- Accusers should use the word "kids" as often as possible when being interviewed.[17]

The ultimate aim of these strategies is to maximize the emotional and media impact of an allegation. The accuser is immediately positioned in an advantageous position, both publicly and litigiously. Meanwhile, the diocese, often unsure of how to respond, is in turn situated in an unflattering and defensive posture.

It has been no secret that the leadership of SNAP has worked closely with a slippery group of attorneys in the last several years,[18] and these attorneys have been frequent attendees at SNAP conferences. It would be no surprise that these lawyers apply these manipulative tactics as well.

The public should be aware of these schemes when it sees the media report such press conferences.

NOTES AND REFERENCES

[1] "Richard McNally Amicus Letter," June 3, 2005. Addressed to Honorable Ronald M. George, Chief Justice and Associate Justices of the California Supreme Court. Re: Nicole Taus vs. Elizabeth Loftus et al. (1st D.C.A. Civ No. A104689, Solano County Superior Court No. FCS02A557). Text at http://ncrj.org/resources/info/mcnally-amicus/

[2] Karen Berkman, "Research finds repressed memories don't exist," ABC News (Australia), September 6, 1010. At http://www.abc.net.au/news/2010-09-06/research-finds-repressed-memories-dont-exist/2250138

[3] Meredith Moran, *My Lie: A True Story of False Memory* (San Francisco: Jossey-Bass), 2010, p. 223.

[4] Berkman, 2010.

[5] Ibid.

[6] Center for Applied Research in the Apostolate, "2010 Annual Report on the Implementation of the Charter for the Protection of Children and Young People," March 2011, page 40. http://www.bishop-accountability.org/usccb/implementation/report_on_2010.pdf

[7] All lists of accused priests can be found at the web site of the Archdiocese of Boston, http://www.bostoncatholic.org/Offices-And-Services/Office-Detail.aspx?id=21314&pid=21606

[8] "Statement of Archbishop Charles Chaput on false charge against deceased priest," Archdiocese of Denver, July 13, 2010. At http://www.archden.org/index.cfm/ID/4207

[9] Vincent Carroll, "Our selective curiosity on sex scandals," *The Denver Post*, October 10, 2010.

[10] The list of accused Los Angeles priests is in "Report to the People of God: Clergy Sexual Abuse, Archdiocese of Los Angeles, 1930-2003," Archdiocese of Los Angeles, February 17, 2004. At http://www.bishop-accountabil-ity.org/usccb/natureandscope/dioceses/reports/losangelesca-rpt.pdf

[11] Rev. Gordon J. MacRae, "Sex Abuse and Signs of Fraud," *Catalyst*, November 2005. At http://www.catholicleague.org/rer.php?topic=The+Sex+Abuse+Scandal&id=109

[12] Mark Hayward, "NH Diocese Will Pay $5 Million to 62 Victims," *Union Leader* (NH), November 27, 2002.

[13] Albert McKeon, "Settlement Reached in Abuse Claims," *The Telegraph* (Nashua, NH), November 27, 2002. From http://www.bishop-accountabil-ity.org/news/2002_11_27_McKeon_SettlementReached.htm.

[14] Hayward, November 27, 2002.

[15] David R. Price, Ph.D., and James J. McDonald, Jr., "The Problem of False Claims of Clergy Sexual Abuse," *Risk Management*, January 2003.

[16] William A. Donohue, PhD., "SNAP Exposed: Unmasking the Survivors Network of those Abused by Priests" (Special Report), August 2011. Available at http://www.catholicleague.org/images/upload/image_201108223332.pdf

[17] Ibid.

[18] I outline some of these relationships in my previous book, *Double Standard*.

10

Defenseless

Despite evidence that indicates their innocence, accused priests often find themselves under brutal attack from zealous lawyers.

Take the case of Fr. Michael Kelly. The California priest, a native of Ireland, had a completely unblemished record in over three decades as a priest until October 2007. A father came forward to claim that Fr. Kelly had abused his son as a 10-year-old in the mid-1980's in the Diocese of Stockton.

The 33-year-old son subsequently came forward and claimed that he had "repressed" the memories of the abuse until 2006.

Fr. Kelly vehemently denied the claim. To assert his innocence, the priest agreed to a polygraph test. The results concluded that he was being completely truthful when he said that he had never abused the boy or anyone else in his entire life.[1]

The diocese was mandated to follow Church protocols, however. It removed the priest from ministry and began to scrutinize the claim. In fact, two separate investigations were conducted: one by the diocese and another by Stockton police.

Neither inspection turned up a shred of evidence against Fr. Kelly.

In addition, when investigators went to question the man and his father about the accusation, they all refused to cooperate and speak with them. The accusers even declined a meeting with the diocese with their lawyer present.[2]

With no evidence or other allegations against Fr. Kelly, the diocese returned the priest to ministry in March 2008.

Yet the crusade against Fr. Kelly continued. The accuser filed a civil suit against the Stockton diocese.

In this case, what may explain the underlying persistence in this case is the lawyer representing Fr. Kelly's accuser. The man's lawyer is Southern California attorney John C. Manly, who has likely pocketed tens of millions of dollars in the past decade suing the Catholic Church.

Unfortunately, Manly is one of the most aggressive lawyers of his type in the country. His track record of twisted facts and untruths is very well established. In fact, in 2006, a Los Angeles Superior Court judge took the rare action of sanctioning Manly for "unacceptable" conduct during a deposition.[3]

Mr. Manly's venom for the Catholic Church cannot be overstated. His penchant for unscrupulousness is problematic, to say the least. Even though Fr. Kelly passed a polygraph test; even though the accuser refused to cooperate with investigators; even though the accuser dubiously claimed that he had "repressed" the memory of the abuse, attorney Manly stated that his client "is the single most credible client I have ever represented."[4]

If Fr. Kelly's flimsy accuser is "the single most credible client" Manly has represented, it certainly makes one wonder about the integrity of the scores of other individuals that the attorney has represented while pocketing his millions.

Then there is the case involving Fr. Czeslaw Szymanski, fondly called "Fr. Chet," from Holy Trinity Parish, a church serving much of the Polish community in Lowell, Massachusetts, a suburb north of Boston.

In December 2010, three men came forward to level accusations of "sexual assault" by Fr. Chet. The men, now in their 30's, allege that the priest "fondled" them between the ages of 6 and 13 in the 1980's.

According to the *Boston Globe*, the men's lawyer, Carmen L. Durso, a veteran litigant against the Church, claims, "Szymanski would fondle the boys in the Holy Trinity Church sacristy before celebrating Mass. He said the alleged sexual abuse continued on a daily basis until 1987."[5]

Needless to say, the claim that these boys were fondled "on a daily basis" in the open view of the sacristy *before Mass* is startling.

In the months following the claims by the original three men, five additional individuals have come forward to attorney Durso to claim impropriety by Fr. Chet.

What does the accused priest have to say about all of this?

Fr. Chet was killed in a car crash on September 24, 1987.

"Credible"

It is a word that most people do not often think about, yet it is a word that those who target the Church find very useful.

Even though a priest may work tirelessly to clear his name after a false accusation, there is often a public spectacle when a diocese returns him to a parish. Although objective information may undoubtedly refute an accusation, those determined to attack the return of a priest will still assert that the pastor received a "credible" allegation of abuse.

Credible simply means "capable of being believed."[6] The media and advocacy groups such as SNAP have powerfully utilized this word when approaching cases of accused priests.

When an accuser comes forward to allege abuse from decades earlier, one can deem the accusation as "credible" simply because the accuser can show that he or she lived at a given time in the same general geographical area of a priest.

Veteran canon lawyer Michael Ritty confirms this. "That level of being 'credible' is a low level of certainty," Ritty told Catholic writer Joe Feuerherd in 2007. "I have seen it as low as the priest happened to be in the [same] parish at the time this person made this allegation – that it was geographically possible. That might have been the only proof [necessary] to go forward."[7]

In other words, unless a person claims that a priest molested him or her on an alien spaceship circling a distant galaxy, one can easily stamp an accusation as "credible."

SNAP frequently utilizes this word to its advantage to lambaste the Church.

For example, in April of 2010, SNAP summoned the media and alarmed churchgoers at Our Lady of Perpetual Help Church in Newhall, California, by claiming that a "credibly accused" cleric had recently been placed in the parish.

The target for SNAP was Msgr. Richard Martini. Until 2003, with over two decades in ministry, no one had ever accused the popular cleric of any wrongdoing whatsoever. Yet a convicted felon serving lengthy time in California's notorious Corcoran State Prison came forward to claim that the monsignor had "fondled" him at a water polo event in the early 1990's. Utilizing former F.B.I. agents and other investigators, the Archdiocese of Los Angeles learned that the accuser's claim was completely without fact. The felon's charge was unsupported "even by [his] own witnesses."[8]

Yet SNAP's frenetic "Southwest Director," Joelle Casteix, descended upon unsuspecting parishioners at Msgr. Martini's new parish to attack the innocent cleric and the Catholic Church. Casteix misleadingly applied the claim that the senior priest had been "credibly accused."[9] Of course, there was very little that was the least bit "credible" about the convicted felon's claim. Yet Casteix's actions caused great confusion, chaos, and hurt among the local parishioners and the community.

Confusion. Chaos. Hurt. This is what the misleading word "credible" can generate when utilized by unscrupulous individuals.

Consumers of media should be very wary of the word "credible" when examining stories of clergy abuse.

NOTES AND REFERENCES

[1] Michael G. Mooney, "Catholic priest placed on leave: He denies allegation he sexually abused boy in the mid-1980's," *The Modesto Bee*, October 12, 2007.

[2] Ken Carlson, "Stockton diocese says no base for abuse allegation, reinstates priest," *The Modesto Bee*, March 15, 2008.

[3] Associated Press, "Attorney sanctioned for behavior during clergy abuse deposition," January 2006.

[4] Carlson, March 2008.

[5] "Victims claim '80s abuse by late Mass. priest," *Boston Globe*, December 9, 2010.

[6] http://dictionary.reference.com/browse/credible

[7] Joe Feuerherd, "Clergy witch hunt? – Due process for accused priests is a sham, critics say," *National Catholic Reporter*, April 25, 2007.

[8] "An Open Letter from the Archdiocese of Los Angeles to the People of Santa Clarita Concerning Msgr. Richard Martini," April 9, 2010. Available at http://www.bishop-accountabil-ity.org/news2010/03_04/2010_04_12_Tidings_AnOpen.htm

[9] SNAP press release, April 11, 2010, "Abuse Victims to Leaflet Parish Where Accused Cleric Will Work," at http://www.snapnetwork.org/snap_press_releases/2010_press_releas-es/041110_abuse_victims_to_leaflet_parish_where_accused_cleric_will_work.htm

CATHOLIC PRIESTS FALSELY ACCUSED

11

SNAP Attacks

One can hardly read a newspaper article or see a television story about the Catholic clergy scandals without a reference or remark from the Illinois-based advocacy group called SNAP, Survivors Network of those Abused by Priests. Its national president, Barbara Blaine, has openly boasted that she has "established a 'network' of reporters in 'all corners of the country' who closely work with SNAP."[1]

While Catholics must continue to demand justice and compassion for real victims of clergy abuse, SNAP's wild actions make it difficult – if not impossible – for faithful Catholics to support the organization. SNAP's public presentations are terribly problematic. When one studies the activities of the group, one sees that SNAP is mean-spirited, misleading, and dishonest.

At one time, some Church officials thought it would be beneficial and charitable to interact with

SNAP. Unfortunately, they only learned the hard way that such gestures are fruitless.

One Church leader who once thought that it would be productive to reach out to SNAP is Archbishop Timothy Dolan. When he was a prelate in Milwaukee years ago, he believed that making himself available to the group would be a constructive expression of support to abuse victims.

He soon learned that such an overture would not be welcomed.

At a contentious visit to a parish in Milwaukee, a member of SNAP *spat in Archbishop Dolan's face.* The member then roared that he would not be silent "until there was a 'going out of business' sign in front of every Catholic parish, church, school and outreach center."

"That's when I knew I should have listened to those who told me that working with them would not be helpful," recalled Archbishop Dolan.[2]

Unfortunately, such relentless mean-spiritedness is part of the fabric of SNAP. The group's tactics are rooted in the aggressive, in-your-face activism formulated by the infamous and influential 1960's radical, Saul Alinsky. Alinsky's tactics are inherently spiteful and vehemently anti-Christian. SNAP's national director, David Clohessy, worked for nearly a decade with the notorious community organization ACORN (Association of Community Organizations for Reform Now), whose nasty strategies were rooted in the theories of Alinsky. (There is much more about the roots of SNAP in my previous book, *Double Standard*.)

SNAP simply does not acknowledge specific cases of false accusations against priests. Never. In the eyes of SNAP, accused priests are still guilty, even if they have been exonerated in a court of law.

For example, in August 2011, a Hawaii jury deliberated just minutes to declare that Fr. Bohdan Borowec, a Ukrainian Catholic priest visiting on vacation from Canada, was entirely innocent on charges of kidnapping and sexual assault stemming from an alleged incident from months earlier.[3]

Fr. Borowec's defense attorney, working pro bono on the case, effectively demonstrated that the claims against the priest were a complete fabrication from a woman of scant credibility. In addition to having an established mental health history, the unstable accuser had a record of making a false accusation against a priest before.

At the trial, the defense also produced e-mails following the alleged incident that demonstrated that the erratic woman was seeking money. These e-mails were exchanged even before she called the police, which she did not do until three days after the incident in question.

In addition, Fr. Borowec had never had any other accusations of wrongdoing against him in decades in ministry.

Yet, despite the complete lack of credibility of the accuser and the fact that a jury quickly acquitted the innocent priest, Joelle Casteix, the agitated "Southwest Director" of SNAP, released a press statement following the case that stated:

Our hearts ache for this brave woman who had the wisdom to report a (sic) horrific crimes to law enforcement. Let's hope that every person who saw, suspected or suffered clergy sex crimes and cover ups in Hawaii – by Borowic or any cleric – will find the courage and strength to speak up, call police, expose wrongdoing, protect kids and start healing.[4]

"Brave woman"? "Horrific crimes"? Of course, there were no "horrific crimes." And the woman was hardly "brave"; the priest's defense showed that the unstable woman had attempted to commit serious fraud.

In the eyes of SNAP, accused priests are guilty – period. Fairness and due process mean very little to the group.

SNAP's press statement again exposed the fact that the group will attempt to bludgeon the Catholic Church by any means necessary, even if it involves attacking innocent people.

[By the way, following the exoneration of Fr. Borowec, the priest's attorney, Shawn A. Luiz, spoke to the *Hawaii Catholic Herald*. Mr. Luiz made a very important point:

"In cases of being falsely accused, the priest's reputation is effectively destroyed while the accuser, on the other hand, enjoys anonymity and suffers no loss of reputation or negative material consequences."[5]

Indeed, Fr. Borowec's rite placed the priest on administrative leave after his arrest, disallowing him from celebrating the liturgy. In addition, the priest was detained for six months in Hawaii, not allowed to return to Canada. Meanwhile, the identity of the accuser was always anonymous.

Attorney Luiz also noted to the paper that while Hawaiian and Canadian media went frenetic over Fr. Borowec's initial arrest months earlier, the coverage of his exoneration was "minimal."[6]]

NOTES AND REFERENCES

[1] Tom McGregor, "Jeff Anderson Uses SNAP to Recruit Sex Abuse Clients," Dallas Blog, April 6, 2010. http://www.dallasblog.com/201004061006346/dallas-blog/jeff-anderson-uses-snap-to-recruit-sex-abuse-clients.html

[2] Serge F. Kovaleski, "Complex Struggle: Prelate's Record in Abuse Crisis," New York Times, May 16, 2010, p. A1.

[3] Patrick Downes, "Visiting Ukrainian rite priest acquitted of assault charges," Hawaii Catholic Herald, August 19, 2011. For more on the case, see www.borowec.com

[4] SNAP press statement, "Priest acquitted; SNAP responds," August 10, 2010. At http://www.snapnetwork.org/snap_statements/2011_statements/081011_priest_acquitted_snap_responds.htm

[5] Downes, August 2010.

[6] Ibid.

CATHOLIC PRIESTS FALSELY ACCUSED

12

SNAP Time

SNAP has claimed that its "primary purpose is to provide support for men and women who have been sexually victimized by members of the clergy."[1] However, with every successive action and press release, it becomes increasingly clear that SNAP's *real* mission is something entirely different.

In September 2011, SNAP paired with a left-wing activist group to petition the International Criminal Court (the ICC, a.k.a. "The Hague") to charge Pope Benedict XVI with "crimes against humanity."

The media promptly trumpeted this story despite the fact that no clear-thinking legal scholar opined that the petition had any merit whatsoever.

For SNAP, the episode was another successful publicity stunt to portray the Catholic Church as a callous cabal that is indifferent to the welfare of children.

Yet the most notable moment of the episode was when *Time* magazine reported the story and quoted SNAP's national director, David Clohessy.

Clohessy told *Time*:

> "We don't think the Pope will be hauled off in handcuffs next week or next month. But by the same token, our long-term chances are excellent."[2]

In other words, the organization's ultimate aim is has nothing to do with the protection of children. It is to see the Pope arrested and the Church weakened.

SNAP's real goal is to smash the Catholic Church.

Attorney Marci A. Hamilton

One of many cagey individuals with whom SNAP has aligned itself is New York attorney Marci A. Hamilton. Hamilton's contempt for the Church is unquestionable. When National Public Radio, CNN, or Comedy Central's *The Daily Show with Jon Stewart* want a guest to bash the Catholic Church, Marci is one they call.

Hamilton is the so-called "Paul R. Verkuil Chair of Public Law" at the Cardozo School of Law at Yeshiva University in New York City. Hamilton has represented SNAP and has done extensive legal work for the organization.

Under the banner of "protecting children," Hamilton has made it her crusade to lobby state legislatures to remove the statute of limitations in order to inflict maximum financial and institutional damage to the Catholic Church. (Statutes of limitations are legal parameters under which a maximum time is set after a crime has occurred for a person to sue civilly or be charged criminally.)

In 2008, Hamilton published a flustered book called *Justice Denied: What America Must Do to Protect Its Children*. Her book attempts to forward her argument that statutes of limitations must be lifted in order to "protect America's children." However, Hamilton's measures are almost singly focused on the Catholic Church. Public institutions – such as schools, where massive abuse and cover-ups are still happening today – appear exempt from Hamilton's wrath. While she claims that lawsuit settlements paid out by public schools would "onerously interfere" with their operations, Hamilton has no concern that similar settlements paid by the Catholic Church would seriously affect its religious, charitable, and educational missions.[3]

Attorney L. Martin Nussbaum and his wife Melissa reviewed the book for an edition of the research periodical, *First Things*. The Nussbaums nabbed Hamilton in a number of outright falsehoods and misleading passages. (For example, Hamilton claimed that, in some states, a child abused at age seven would have only until the age of nine to sue the abuser. That is simply false in all 50 states and the District of Columbia.[4])

The Nussbaums concluded:

Marci Hamilton's Justice Denied *is a sloppy piece of work, poorly researched and poorly written. It is a diatribe against the Catholic Church disguised as a solution to child sexual abuse. Hamilton's clients and ours – all of us – deserve better.*[5]

Lest one think that the Nussbaums' review is simply retaliation for harsh criticism of the Catholic Church, one can learn that other works by Hamilton have not fared well in the fact-checking department either. A professional journal review of Hamilton's 2005 book, *God vs. the Gavel*, is so resoundingly negative, it has become somewhat legendary in scholarly circles for its harsh, scathing assessment.

Writing for a 2007 edition of the *Michigan Law Review*, University of Virginia law professor Douglas Laycock entitled his review of Hamilton's book, "A Syllabus of Errors." In a nearly 20-page (!) critique of the work, Laycock cites page after page of errors in fact and legal analysis by Hamilton.

Dr. Laycock lambastes Hamilton's book as "poorly executed," "disorganized," "self-contradictory," and "riddled with errors." Tagging it as a "dreadful book," the professor adds, "Elsewhere I have praised Hamilton's judgment, but this time there is nothing good to say."[6]

Here is Dr. Laycock's closing remarks from his review:

Occasional errors are inevitable, but here the extraordinary number of errors, often with reference to famous cases and basic doctrines, implies a reckless disregard for truth. I document these errors for a reason. No one should cite this book. No one should rely on it for any purpose ...

IV. Conclusion

Legal scholars may be advocates, and they may reach out to nonscholarly audiences, but every scholar has a minimum obligation of factual accuracy and intellectual honesty. God vs. the Gavel *does not come close to meeting either standard. Nor does it offer a sustained argument for its legal claim about the institutional competence of courts and legislatures. Its many footnotes offer the patina of scholarship, but there is no substance of scholarship. This book is unworthy of the Cambridge University Press and the Benjamin N. Cardozo School of Law.*[7]

File under: "Marci Hamilton: A reckless disregard for truth."

NOTES AND REFERENCES

[1] SNAP, IRS Form 990, 2008.

[2] Stephan Faris, "Could the Vatican Go to Court for Human-Rights Abuses?" *Time*, September 20, 2011.

[3] L. Martin Nussbaum and Melissa Nussbaum, "MarciWorld," *First Things*, February 5, 2009.

[4] Ibid.

[5] Ibid.

[6] Douglas Laycock, "A Syllabus of Errors," *Michigan Law Review*, April 2007: Vol. 107:1169-1187.

[7] Ibid.

13

BishopAccountability.org

Another organization which the media enjoys to seek in stories about the Catholic Church is a group called BishopAccountability.org. BishopAccountability.org is a reliable source for journalists who desire quotations to lambaste the Catholic Church.

BishopAccountability.org is a high-profile web site purporting to catalog the Catholic Church abuse narrative. Unlike SNAP, it does not claim to provide any actual support for abuse victims.

BishopAccountability.org's primary function is posting information. The main feature of the site is its enormous database of "publicly accused" Catholic priests. It largely posts news articles about priests' cases, and it also provides items such as Church documents and court filings (some of which appear to have been dubiously obtained).

According to the group's 2009 IRS Form 990, the organization pocketed over $300,000. Of that, its president, a crafty individual by the name of Terence W. McKiernan, took home compensation of over $83,000. It also claimed to spend over $34,000 on "consultants," $36,600 on "archive expenses," and almost $14,300 on travel.[1]

Although the organization claims that it does not seek to undermine the authority of the Church, this assertion rings hollow. The group's own words and actions reveal a gang that is on par with SNAP in its venom for the Catholic Church. In fact, the two organizations have closely collaborated on a number of occasions over the years.

Anne Barrett Doyle is a high-profile director at BishopAccountability.org. Her history of public protests against the Catholic Church has been very well documented. For many years Doyle has been deeply involved with several "reform" groups (read: dissident), including the notorious Voice of the Faithful.

In the contentious year of 2002, Doyle was an active and visible presence at several high-profile Sunday protests at Boston-area churches. One blogger reported that Doyle attempted to disrupt a healing service at Mission Church in Roxbury.[2]

At the same church, Doyle also allegedly accosted an elderly woman who was outside the church quietly praying the Rosary by herself while waiting for a ride.

According to a witness, "Doyle, apparently enraged at the lady's quiet display of piety, marched up to her and loudly proclaimed, 'I could introduce you to the mother of a victim of a priest who hung himself with a rosary just like the one you're using!'" (When the witness asked Doyle to produce this alleged mother, "Doyle was unable to do so." "I pray [the elderly woman] has forgotten the incident," the witness has written.)[3]

The fact that Doyle apparently chose to verbally berate a pious woman who was silently praying reveals a lot about her true feelings. The incident suggests that Doyle has no respect for people who adhere to traditional Church practices.

In 2003, the *Boston Globe* profiled the angry Doyle. In the article Doyle flouted the fact that she was reveling in a dinner of beef stew on a Friday during Lent. According to the paper, her deliberate rejection of the Church discipline of refraining from meat on Fridays in Lent was her way of expressing her "profound disillusionment with the leadership of her church (sic)."[4] (Completely lost on the self-absorbed Doyle was the fact that the abstention of meat on Friday has nothing to do with *her* and everything to do with Jesus Christ.)

Doyle has collaborated with SNAP in several endeavors over the years. In 2011, she appeared and spoke at the group's annual conference. (It was not the first time she had done so.) According to an exclusive report by the Catholic League, Doyle railed against the Church regarding the abuse scandals and claimed "the conspiracy begins at the Vatican."

"That's right," Dr. William Donohue, president of the Catholic League, replied in his report. "She believes that Rome is at the heart of a world-wide *conspiracy* to protect molesting priests."[5]

Meanwhile, BishopAccountability.org is maintained primarily by its president McKiernan.

McKiernan also spoke aggressively at SNAP's 2011 conference. BishopAccountability.org's chief revealed his true colors when he said, "I hope we can find ways of sticking it to [New York Archbishop Timothy M. Dolan]," the president of the United States Conference of Catholic Bishops. He berated the leader as a "doctrinal enforcer" who "only cares about climbing the ladder." McKiernan then leveled the shocking charge, without any supporting evidence whatsoever, that the archbishop is "keeping the lid on 55 names" of abusive priests under his watch.[6]

Asked later by a writer for *Our Sunday Visitor*, a Catholic newsweekly, to respond to the comments he had made, McKiernan said that he may have been "too opinionated" in his remarks about Archbishop Dolan, yet he stood by his claim about the 55 priests.[7]

(McKiernan's claim about the 55 priests begs the question: Why doesn't McKiernan simply publish the 55 names and/or give the list to the New York archbishop? "Not a single person in the entire country has ever made such a scurrilous accusation," wrote Dr. Donohue. "It's time to either put up or shut up."[8])

The most troubling aspect of BishopAccountability.org, however, is the duplicity with which it operates. The organization demonstrates little care about the integrity or veracity of the accusations against priests that it publicly posts. It will do everything in its power to display as much information as it can about accused priests on its site, even in cases in which a priest is found to be totally innocent.

For example, an accuser can invoke the discredited claim of "repressed memory" and lodge an abuse complaint against a long-dead priest who had no other allegations against him. The organization will still make every effort to catalog the case and publish the priest's name *and picture* in its database of "publicly accused" priests.

This is exactly what the organization did with Michigan's Monsignor John Slowey, who died in 1983. A man came forward in 2009 to say he had somehow "repressed" the memory of being abused *over five decades earlier* at age 5 or 6. He claimed he had only recently "recovered" the memory of it happening. Msgr. Slowey never had any other accusations against him.[9] (By the way, even though the diocese *denied* the allegations and asserted that they were unsubstantiated, it *still* paid a $225,000 settlement to the accuser.[10])

To wit, no clear-thinking individual would believe for one second that either of the two accusations against Los Angeles' Roger Cardinal Mahony are the least bit credible. (See Chapter 8.) Yet the former archbishop is plastered on the site like a child molester. If one visits BishopAccountability.org, one will find Cardinal Mahony in its extensive database of "publicly accused" priests. The site post the cardinal's name and picture, and the ominous word "Accused" is stamped alongside. In the "notes" column of his entry, the site has printed, "Accused of abuse."[11]

And despite the claim on its site that it will not post the cases of priests in which accusers have recanted their claims, BishopAccountability.org still does so. For example, in the case of Louisiana's Monsignor Ray Hebert (see Chapter 1), the accusers' lawyers filed a claim in court that unequivocally stated that the cleric "did not molest their clients." Yet BishopAccountability.org still prominently lists Msgr. Hebert as "Sued" on its site.[12]

Is there honesty and "accountability" from BishopAccountability.org? Not at all.

According to a news article, McKiernan has claimed to be an "orthodox Catholic."[13] Yet one cannot help but question this when one observes such a public disregard for the Eighth Commandment ("You shall not bear false witness against your neighbor.")

The public should be aware that BishopAccountability.org is not just some innocent organization that simply seeks to catalog cases of abusive priests. Like SNAP, its mission is far more nefarious. It seeks to bludgeon the Catholic Church as much as it can.

NOTES AND REFERENCES

[1] BishopAccountability.org is registered in Massachusetts. Its recent filings can be obtained through the Office of the Attorney General of Massachusetts.

[2] Domenico Bettinelli Jr., "Kelly Clark on the 'Ode to Anne Barrett Doyle'," Bettnet.com, http://www.bettnet.com/blog/index.php/weblog/comments/kelly_clark_on_the_ode_to_anne_barrett_doyle/

[3] Ibid.

[4] Eileen McNamara, "Still Catholic, but changed," *Boston Globe*, March 9, 2003.

[5] William A. Donohue, PhD., "SNAP Exposed: Unmasking the Survivors Network of those Abused by Priests" (Special Report), August 2011. Available at http://www.catholicleague.org/images/upload/image_20110822 3332.pdf

[6] Ibid.

[7] Brian Fraga, "Report questions motives of clerical sex abuse victims' groups," *Our Sunday Visitor*, September 11, 2011. At http://www.osv.com/tabid/7621/itemid/8341/Report-questions-motives-of-clerical-sex-abuse-vic.aspx

[8] Donohue, August 2011.

[9] See the listing at http://bishop-accountability.org/priestdb/PriestDBbylastName-S.html

[10] Kathleen Lavey, "Lansing Catholic Diocese Paid $225,000 to Settle Abuse Claim Against Deceased Monsignor," Lansing State Journal, August 25, 2010.

[11] See the listing at http://bishop-accountability.org/priestdb/PriestDBbylastName-M.html

[12] See the listing at http://bishop-accountability.org/priestdb/PriestDBbylastName-H.html

[13] Fraga, September 2011.

CATHOLIC PRIESTS FALSELY ACCUSED

14

Philadelphia:
No Brotherly Love

"The grand jury process itself is largely devoid of legal rules. The process has become one that wholly fails to protect ordinary American citizens. The balance has shifted so dramatically in favor of the prosecution that it has been noted, time and again, that 'A good prosecutor could get a grand jury to indict a ham sandwich'." – Kyle O'Dowd, Legislative Director, National Association of Criminal Defense Lawyers (NACDL), 2000.[1]

Like Boston nine years earlier, the city of Philadelphia in 2011 became a geographical focal point for the issue of Catholic clergy abuse.

Although two previous grand jury reports against the Catholic Church over the previous eight years did not result in any recommendations for criminal charges, Philadelphia District Attorney R. Seth Williams convened a third grand jury in 2010 to investigate claims of abuse in the Catholic Church.

In February 2011, the grand jury released its findings in a stunning report.

The report floored Catholics and non-Catholics alike with the claim that there was "substantial evidence" that 37 "credibly accused" abusive priests were serving in active ministry in the Philadelphia area. The report portrayed the archdiocese as a callous organization that was indifferent, if not hostile, to the plight of clergy abuse victims.[2]

The report brought various felony charges against five individuals: one active priest, a restricted priest, a former priest, a former lay teacher, and an active monsignor.

This news astonished the city of Philadelphia and stunned the Archdiocese of Philadelphia.

People asked: With so many safeguards and audits in place, how could such mistakes still be happening in 2011?

However, there was another question that observers could have been asking but were not: Were the claims in the grand jury report actually *true*?

There were good reasons to challenge many of the shocking claims in the scathing report.

For example, the grand jury report slammed Philadelphia Church officials for the manner with which they investigated claims of abuse by accusers. The report boldly asserted that the Church in Philadelphia routinely "conducted non-investigations that predictably failed to establish priests' guilt."

In other words, the grand jury suggested that the archdiocese let molesters "run wild" in its diocese, and the Church's investigations of abuse had the predetermined goal of establishing priests' innocence.

However, this assertion is firmly refuted by a look at some facts. The Archdiocese of Philadelphia in fact investigated *numerous* cases of abuse in the previous several years. In an alarming number of cases it determined abuse to be founded and recommended that clerics be laicized. In fact, for a number of years now, the Philadelphia archdiocese has maintained a high-profile web page that publicly posts the names, pictures, and assignments of the many clerics whom the archdiocese has found to be guilty of abuse. The list is extensive and spans the removal of priests over the past several decades. The most recent count of listed priests is 64.[3]

So the grand jury's claim that the archdiocese had "conducted non-investigations" is not only unfair, but untrue. The archdiocese, in compliance with the 2002 Dallas Charter, employed a review board – composed not just of clerics, but a team of experienced psychologists and child victim advocates – to aggressively and vigorously investigate claims of abuse brought to its attention. It was the job of the review board to investigate claims of abuse and arrive at recommendations for action. Since its inception, the board has included individuals as "health-care providers with expertise in child abuse, a clinical psychologist who treats sexual-abuse victims, social workers with experience in child welfare, a family-law attorney, a county probations officer, a private investigator, and a pastor. Two members are survivors of child sexual abuse, one by a priest. Most board members are parents."[4]

Contrary to public perception, the Philadelphia review board was quite aggressive in its duties. In a number of instances, a priest did not even have to commit abuse to be removed. Ana Maria Catanzaro, president of the review board, has stated, "In several cases, we could not say that a priest's inappropriate actions violated [canonical] norms, but we still determined that the matter was serious enough to recommend his permanent removal."[5]

In other words, the review board appeared to take a very strict approach towards clerical misconduct. If the board found that a priest seriously violated his vows, it recommended his removal. In fact, the board recommended removal of the priest in most of the cases it reviewed.[6]

Yet the grand jury amazingly publicized an entirely opposite portrait of the review board. While the review board envisioned itself as dedicated group of child advocates that was determined to find the truth and act accordingly, the grand jury portrayed it as a callous and uncaring gang that zealously fought to defend the Church from scandal. The grand jury actually stated, "In cases where the archdiocese's review board has made a determination, the results have often been even worse than no decision at all."[7]

Responding to this statement, Ms. Catanzaro reported, "That sweeping judgment stunned review-board members."[8]

Ms. Catanzaro also had a serious objection to the grand jury's approach, "The grand jury never asked us to testify about how we arrived at recommendations."[9]

That, indeed, is an eye-raising fact. If the grand jury sought an honest inquiry into how the Archdiocese of Philadelphia looked into cases of abuse, it seems suspicious that the group did not seek to question the archdiocesan review board. The experienced panel had investigated the very same cases that the jury was examining.

Quite simply, it seems that in cases that the review board found the abuse to be uncorroborated, self-refuting, or not credible, the grand jury took the accusations at full face value.

NOTES AND REFERENCES

[1] Kyle O'Dowd, Legislative Director, National Association of Criminal Defense Lawyers (NACDL) 2000. www.nacdl.org

[2] Report of the Grand Jury, "In the Court of Common Pleas, First Judicial District of Philadelphia, Criminal Trial Division," January 2011.
http://www.phila.gov/districtattorney/PDFs/clergyAbuse2-finalReport.pdf

3 A list of these priests is listed at the website of the Archdiocese of Philadelphia,
http://archphila.org/protection/Updates/update_main.htm

4 Ana Maria Catanzaro, "The Fog of Scandal," *Commonweal*, June 17, 2011.

5 Ibid.

6 John P. Martin, "Members of Philadelphia archdiocesan abuse panel counter criticism," *Philadelphia Inquirer*, February 13, 2011.

7 Report of the Grand Jury, January 2011.

8 Catanzaro, June 17, 2011.

9 Ibid.

15

The Philadelphia – SNAP Connection

One interesting (yet unreported) element of the Philadelphia clergy abuse narrative has been the fact that members of the Philadelphia District Attorney's Office and leaders of SNAP have collaborated very closely over the years.

Could the intensity with which the Philadelphia D.A.'s Office has relentlessly pursued the Catholic Church be the result of its associations with SNAP?

At first, such a question may sound paranoidal and unwarranted. However, a number of eye-opening episodes cause concern that the Catholic Church has not received equitable justice and scrutiny under the law in Philadelphia. For example:

1. In 2006, when John Salveson, the long-time president of the Philadelphia chapter of SNAP, decided to form his own victim advocacy organization, among his first actions was to assign a woman named Mariana Sorensen to his board of directors.[1]

Who is Mariana Sorensen? She is a veteran Assistant District Attorney in Philadelphia. She was the lead author of both the 2005 and 2011 grand jury reports, both of which contained significant content about the Catholic Church that was not only mean-spirited, but misleading and false.

In an ardent 2006 opinion article for the *Philadelphia Inquirer*, Sorensen argued for lifting the statute of limitations for abuse claims. Yet her desire for this legislation seemed almost singly rooted in her eagerness to punish the Catholic Church.[2] (Lifting statutes of limitations = more opportunities for lawsuits against the Catholic Church.)

Also in 2006, Sorensen co-wrote a nasty letter to then-Cardinal Justin Rigali of the Archdiocese of Philadelphia, recklessly accusing the archbishop of being callous and uncaring in light of priests committing "countless child rapes."[3]

It is certainly not a stretch to say that Sorensen, the prosecutor in the 2011-2012 Philadelphia criminal cases against Catholic clergy, has a deep animus against the Catholic Church.

2. Yeshiva University law professor Marci A. Hamilton is a lawyer who has worked extensively with SNAP over the years. Her distaste for the Church has been very well-documented.

The Philadelphia – SNAP Connection

On September 25, 2007, Hamilton convened a conference in New York City ("Call to Action") with the purpose of advancing legislative efforts to lift statutes of limitations for abuse claims in states across the country.

As witnessed on a video of the conference, Hamilton introduced current and former leaders of SNAP, including Barbara Blaine, the founder and president of SNAP; and Philadelphia's John Salveson.

Hamilton then introduced two members of the Philadelphia District Attorney's Office who had joined her for her efforts that day. She prefaced her introduction of the individuals by saying that the Philadelphia District Attorney's Office "has been – by far – the best D.A.'s office in the country."[4]

One of the two prosecutors was – no surprise – Mariana Sorensen. The other was Charles F. Gallagher III, then-Philadelphia's Deputy District Attorney.

So here was a lawyer for SNAP openly praising Philadelphia as "the best D.A.'s office in the country." Why?

Certainly the answer lies in the animus with which Philadelphia has gone after the Catholic Church.

3. An October 13, 2006, forum at Temple University School of Law convened to discuss the "aftermath" of the 2005 Philadelphia grand jury report against the Catholic Church. Featured speakers on the panel included:
- Lynne Abraham, then-District Attorney of Philadelphia;
- Marci Hamilton;

- John Salveson (the former head of SNAP Philadelphia);
- Maureen McCartney, a former Assistant District Attorney of Philadelphia (who worked with Mariana Sorenson in Philly's 2003-2005 investigation of the Church. McCartney co-wrote that nasty 2006 letter with Sorenson to then-Archbishop of Philadelphia Justin Cardinal Rigali).

Leaders of SNAP Philadelphia were also reportedly present at this collaborative event.[5]

4. An August 5, 2008, panel – presented in part by SNAP – convened at the Siegel Jewish Community Center in Wilmington, Delaware, to discuss – again – legislative efforts to lift statutes of limitations. Featured speakers included:
- Charles Gallagher, Deputy D.A. of Philadelphia;
- Marci Hamilton, law professor and SNAP attorney; and
- Joelle Casteix, "Southwest Director" of SNAP.[6]

5. In August 2011, the Catholic League for Religious and Civil Rights released an exclusive report about the speakers at the annual national conference for SNAP, which took place a month earlier in Washington D.C.

William Spade, a former District Attorney in Philadelphia, was one of the event's speakers.

According to the League's report, in an angry address, Spade described Cardinal Justin Rigali, at the time the outgoing Archbishop of Philadelphia, as "cagey and wily."

Spade then, in the words of the report, said that when he was in the Philly D.A.'s Office, "the man he wanted to get more than anyone else" was Cardinal Anthony Bevilacqua, the former Archbishop of Philadelphia. Spade then made an alarming claim that Cardinal Bevilacqua's niece and her husband, who are both physicians, "concocted" a diagnosis of dementia so that the former archbishop would not be criminally indicted and forced to testify in court. Not surprisingly, Spade did not provide any evidence for his astonishing claim.[7]

The bottom line is that members of the Philadelphia District Attorney's Office and leaders at SNAP have worked together for a long time.

While this unseemly partnership may not be illegal, it surely helps to explain the extreme hostility and acrimony with which Philadelphia has relentlessly pursued the Catholic Church over the years. With *three* grand jury reports in the last decade (not just two, as widely reported), the Philadelphia D.A.'s Office has not targeted any other organization for its past abuses with the same prosecutorial zeal. Not – even – close.

It should also be noted that nearby jurisdictions in Pennsylvania have not identified wrongdoing in the Church to the extent that Philadelphia has.

For example, in August 2011, the Pittsburgh District Attorney's Office – just a stone's throw away from

Philadelphia in a sense – closed a criminal inquiry against the Church after it determined "none of the allegations merited criminal prosecution."[8]

How is it that one city can claim to find so much criminal wrongdoing while a nearby jurisdiction concludes that it finds nothing?

Has the Catholic Church in Philadelphia received equitable scrutiny and fair treatment under the law?

Events in the City of Brotherly Love certainly prompt these questions.

NOTES AND REFERENCES

[1] Dave Pierre, "Evidence of Collaboration Between the Philadelphia District Attorney's Office and SNAP," TheMediaReport.com, August 2011. http://www.themediareport.com/aug2011/philadelphia-da-snap-collaboration.htm

[2] Mariana C. Sorensen, "One year on, no fix in abuse laws," *Philadelphia Inquirer*, September 28, 2006.

[3] A copy of the letter is viewable at my website, TheMediaReport.com, http://www.themediareport.com/aug2011/Sorensen-McCartney-072606-letter-Card-Rigali.pdf

[4] A video of the event is viewable through TheMediaReport.com, "Evidence of Collaboration Between the Philadelphia District Attorney's Office and SNAP," August 2011. http://www.themediareport.com/aug2011/philadelphia-da-snap-collaboration.htm

[5] Dave Pierre, "Evidence of Collaboration Between the Philadelphia District Attorney's Office and SNAP (Part II)," TheMediaReport.com, August 2011.
http://www.themediareport.com/aug2011/part-ii-philadelphia-da-snap-collaboration.htm

[6] Ibid.

[7] William A. Donohue, PhD., "SNAP Exposed: Unmasking the Survivors Network of those Abused by Priests" (Special Report), August 2011. Available at
http://www.catholicleague.org/images/upload/image_20110822 3332.pdf

[8] John P. Martin, "Pittsburgh D.A. ends clergy abuse inquiry," *Philadelphia Inquirer*, August 14, 2011.

CATHOLIC PRIESTS FALSELY ACCUSED

16

Fr. Joseph DiGregorio, Archdiocese of Philadelphia

As an example of a case that supposedly contained "substantial evidence" of abuse, the 2011 Philadelphia grand jury report profiled the case of Rev. Joseph L. DiGregorio, a priest who had served over four decades in ministry.

Fr. DiGregorio's record as a pastor was unblemished until a woman came forward in 2005 to accuse the cleric of forcefully molesting her nearly forty years earlier, in "1967 or 1968." The review board spent well over a year examining his case. In 2006 the board concluded that "evidence obtained through the investigative process was not sufficient to substantiate" the single allegation against the cleric. With no other complaints against the pastor, it recommended that Fr. DiGregorio return to ministry.

Yet the grand jury report took strong issue with the archdiocese's decision to allow Fr. DiGregorio back to work. The report cited the case of Fr. DiGregorio as another example of how the archdiocese had supposedly recklessly returned a "credibly accused" molester back into an environment where he supposedly could harm minors again.

The fact that Fr. DiGregorio had only a single, dubious complaint over such a long period of time did not seem to matter to the grand jury. The fact that the alleged incident took place nearly four decades earlier did not factor into its opinion either.

And, most astonishingly, the grand jury arrived at its conclusion without even interviewing Fr. DiGregorio. The grand jury never subpoenaed the cleric. Neither did it ask him to testify or provide a statement to give his version of events. For the grand jury, the uncorroborated testimony of the single accuser was enough to slam Fr. DiGregorio and the archdiocesan review board for "callousness."[1]

Bowing to intense public pressure following the release of the grand jury report, the Archdiocese of Philadelphia rapidly re-suspended Fr. DiGregorio (along with two other priests the report profiled).

Yet rather than taking his suspension and negative publicity lying down, Fr. DiGregorio aggressively went to the media to declare his innocence. On February 18, 2011, the priest appeared live on *The Dom Giordano Show* on Talk Radio WPHT 1210AM.

With a number of local television stations gathered at the radio station to record his appearance, Fr.

Fr. Joseph DiGregorio

DiGregorio took strong exception to the claims about his case that had been aired in the grand jury report and in the media. For starters, an article about his case in the *Philadelphia Inquirer* didn't even identify his name correctly. (It named him as Fr. "Stephen" DiGregorio, not Joseph.)

Speaking over the airwaves, Fr. DiGregorio strongly professed his innocence.[2]

> "I have not in my whole life ever, ever, ever acted in an inappropriate way – not only with a child, but with anybody. Period.

> "Every statement [the accuser] made concerning me is an absolute lie, completely and totally a lie. I never once touched her. I never once groped her or did anything inappropriate. I was never in her company alone. The only times I saw her was when she came to the rectory to see [another priest].

> "In my almost 45 years of me being a priest my character and integrity have never been questioned. Almost 20 of those 45 years were spent as an army chaplain in the United States Army. I was deployed in Operation Desert Shield, Desert Storm for almost a year, and again in Operation Iraqi Freedom for 10 months.

> "I love my country, I love my Church. I am not intimidated by false accusations against my character. I am, however, angry – very angry – and I intend to fight these accusations with every legal means at my disposal."

Fr. DiGregorio then cited a number of glaring inconsistencies in his accuser's allegations. For example, as the priest stated, "In the original allegation the young woman in question states I touched her once in an inappropriate manner. [Yet years later, she claimed] that I repeatedly touched and groped her.

"Perhaps some memory-awakening drug was administered," said the priest. "I categorically stated then as I do now that I never touched her in any manner whatsoever."

In addition, Fr. DiGregorio went on to state that he totally understands the anger people have felt in recent years over the despicable stories of abuse at the hands of Catholic clergy.

"I sympathize totally with the victims of sexual abuse, especially those by priests," the priest continued over the airwaves. "I sympathize with them entirely. If a priest has done something wrong, and is credibly proven that he did, he should be punished. I'm the first to have said that. I said that consistently when I was in the army."

Fr. DiGregorio's appearance on *The Dom Giordano Show* concluded with phone calls from listeners into the show.

Many callers voiced support for the priest. Those who have been parishioners under his watch testified to the man's integrity.

"I don't believe any of it," a caller, Linda, said of the accusations against her one-time priest.

As Fr. DiGregorio listened to the words of encouragement from listeners, he was moved to tears.

NOTES AND REFERENCES

[1] Report of the Grand Jury, "In the Court of Common Pleas, First Judicial District of Philadelphia, Criminal Trial Division," January 2011.
http://www.phila.gov/districtattorney/PDFs/clergyAbuse2-finalReport.pdf

[2] Audiotape on file. *The Dom Giordano Show*, WPHT 1210AM, February 18, 2011.

CATHOLIC PRIESTS FALSELY ACCUSED

17

The Double Standard Continues

On Saturday, February 19, 2011, the *Los Angeles Times* published a news article, "Ex-high school principal gets 8 years for molesting four girls." The case involved Jonas Vital Silverio, 41, who had pleaded no contest to 10 counts of lewd acts on a child 14 or 15 years old. His crimes spanned over a decade and may have involved scores of victims.

At the hearing for his sentencing, victims and families spoke emotionally of the deep harm that Silverio wreaked upon them.

"This man has stained my childhood forever," one victim said. "Because of him, I do not trust anybody."

"I went to him for help in his office once," the young woman added. "I ended up on the floor with him lying on top trying to kiss me."

But buried in the middle of the article was an alarming fact, even though the paper presented this troubling detail in just a passing manner:

> Prosecutor Stephanie Chavez said Silverio had a history of sexual misconduct.
>
> In 1995, Silverio was placed on probation for a misdemeanor conviction of unlawful sexual intercourse with a minor.[1]

In other words, Silverio was serving openly as the lead administrator of a high school even though he had a *criminal record* for *sex with a minor*. This was jaw-dropping information that other local outlets did not even include.

Media outside of Los Angeles barely recorded this stomach-turning case. Surely if this case involved a Catholic priest or bishop, it is not hard to imagine that many more media outlets would have covered this story. It likely would have garnered national attention. And surely writers would have framed the story in a manner to maximize embarrassment to the Church. It is not too hard to imagine the headlines:

> - "Catholic Church allowed convicted child sex offender to molest kids again"
> - "Criminal child molester found haven in Catholic Church."

Just a week before this shocking school story, the *New York Times* forcefully investigated a case involving a Catholic priest across the country in California who had admitted to an unlawful relationship with a 16-year-old girl back in 1966, *45 years earlier*. Despite the fact that the priest had no other accusations since then, the paper posted a trove of documents related to the case.[2]

Many media venues picked up on the story, and the narrative was widely reported.

Yet the *New York Times* and most other major media outlets did not find the story of the child-molesting high school principal with a criminal record worth reporting.

The case of the molesting principal is hardly an anomaly. The truth is that abuses and cover-ups are *rampant* in our public schools today.

In December 2010, the United States General Accounting Office (GAO) released a shocking report chronicling eye-opening abuses and cover-ups in our nation's schools. The GAO alarmingly reported:

- "Individuals with histories of sexual misconduct were hired or retained by public and private schools as teachers";
- "schools allowed offenders with histories of targeting children to obtain or continue employment"; and
- "offenders used their new positions as school employees or volunteers to abuse more children after they were hired."[3]

In other words, this recent GAO report detailed exactly what officials in the Catholic Church have been criticized for doing decades ago. Yet the reporting in the media about these awful crimes happening *today* in public schools was nearly nonexistent. Only a handful of news outlets touched the story. (Yes, the *New York Times* was again nowhere to be found on this one.)

And, unfortunately, this was not the first time that the media turned a dismissive eye to sickening callousness in our neighborhood schools.

In 2004, the Department of Education released a report authored by Hofstra University professor Charol Shakeshaft. Entitled "Educator Sexual Misconduct: A Synthesis of Existing Literature," the report thoroughly examined the widespread problem of child sexual abuse by teachers in our nation's public schools.

Harmonizing a number of large-sample studies, Dr. Shakeshaft concluded that "more than 4.5 million students are subject to sexual misconduct by an employee of a school sometime between kindergarten and 12th grade."[4] Startlingly, in the very next sentence she wrote, "Possible limitations of the study would all suggest that the findings reported here *under-estimate* educator sexual misconduct in schools" (emphasis added). The professor also went on to add, "[A 2003 report] that nearly 9.6 percent of students are targets of educator sexual misconduct sometime during their school career presents the most accurate data available at this time."[5] There are roughly 50 million students in America's public schools.

The Double Standard Continues

Dr. Shakeshaft has concluded that just between the years 1991 and 2000, United States educators sexually victimized 290,000 innocent children.[6] (By contrast, a total of about 11,000 individuals allege abuse by Catholic clergy dating back to 1950.[7])

There was also an explosive section in Dr. Shakeshaft's report discussing the consequences (or lack thereof) of known abusers in public schools. The professor reported, "In an early [1994] study of 225 cases of educator sexual abuse in New York, all of the accused had admitted to sexual abuse of a student but none of the abusers was reported to authorities."[8]

That is an important and alarming piece of information. Here is a visual of that startling statistic:

Number of abusive educators: **225**
Number reported to police: **0**

So, in other words, as recently as 1994, it was the *universal* practice in New York among school administrators not to call police to report abusers.

In addition, that same cited 1994 study reported that only *1 percent* of those abusive educators lost their licenses to teach. In addition, most amazingly, "25 percent received *no consequence* or were reprimanded informally and off-the-record. Nearly 39 percent chose to leave the district, *most with positive recommendations* or even retirement packages intact" (emphasis added).[9]

By all measures, these practices in New York would be defined as a "widespread cover-up."

CATHOLIC PRIESTS FALSELY ACCUSED

Three years later, in October 2007, the Associated Press published a stunning three-part series on sex abuse in public schools. After seven months of research it "found 2,570 educators whose teaching credentials were revoked, denied, surrendered or sanctioned from 2001 through 2005 following allegations of sexual misconduct." The series documented the widespread practice of "passing the trash," in which criminally abusive teachers remain unpunished and are surreptitiously moved from one unsuspecting school to another. The report defined such teachers as "mobile molesters."[10]

Also included in the AP series was the sickening case of a teacher who kidnapped "more than 20 girls, some as young as 9. Among other things, he told prosecutors that he put rags in the girls' mouths, taped them shut and also bound their hands and feet with duct tape and rope for his own sexual stimulation."[11]

Not only did the AP chronicle a number of nauseating reports of abuse, it cataloged how the court system opposes victims who seek damages for the harm they have suffered. Unlike the Catholic Church, corporations, and other institutions, public schools have a special immunity from being sued in most abuse cases. Courts have ruled that unless a victim can prove that a school district undoubtedly *knew* that a teacher was a molester, there are no grounds for a lawsuit.

For example, the state of Pennsylvania sentenced a teacher to up to 31 years in state prison after it was discovered that the educator repeatedly had sex with a 12-year-old girl, a student of his. The family filed a civil suit against the school district, but a federal judge dismissed the case, "saying administrators had no obligation to protect her from a predatory teacher since officials were unaware of the abuse, despite what the court called widespread 'unsubstantiated rumors' in the school."

"The system fails hundreds of kids each year," the investigation concluded.[12]

Yet again, the American media was largely silent. Neither the *Boston Globe*, the *New York Times*, nor the *Los Angeles Times* touched the AP series. There were no angry demands that school districts establish "abuse panels" or that administrators "be held accountable" for "harboring pedophiles."

One can only wonder if the words *priest, bishop*, or *Cardinal* were in any of these cases, these papers would have acted differently.

[Author note: Many readers may have noticed that the second half of this chapter consists of some material from my previous book, *Double Standard*. I felt that this information was essential to repeat. A bit of material from *Double Standard* can also be found in Chapter 19. Thank you.]

NOTES AND REFERENCES

[1] Shan Li, "Ex-high school principal gets 8 years for molesting four girls." *Los Angeles Times*, February 19, 2011.

2 Jennifer Medina, "Los Angeles Archdiocese to Dismiss Priest Over Admission of Molesting Girl," *New York Times*, February 12, 2011, p. A12.

3 "K-12 Education: Selected Cases of Public and Private Schools That Hired or Retained Individuals with Histories of Sexual Misconduct," United States Government Accountability Office, GAO-11-200 December 8, 2010.

4 Charol Shakeshaft, "Educator Sexual Misconduct: A Synthesis of Existing Literature," U.S. Department of Education, June 2004.

5 Ibid.

6 George Weigel, "Church gets an unfair rap: Pope has been at forefront of change," *Philadelphia Inquirer*, April 4, 2010.

7 John Jay College of Criminal Justice, "The Nature and Scope of the Problem of Sexual Abuse of Minors by Catholic Priests and Deacons in the United States," 2004.

8 Shakeshaft, June 2004.

9 Ibid.

10 Associated Press, "Sexual misconduct plagues U.S. schools: Survey finds 2,500 incidents over 5 years, across all types of districts," October 20, 2007. At http://www.msnbc.msn.com/id/21392345/ns/us_news-education/

11 Ibid.

12 Ibid.

18

Kathy Told a Story

In 2005, an Irish woman named Kathy O'Beirne released her book, *Kathy's Story: The True Story of a Childhood Hell Inside the Magdalen Laundries*.[1] The tome details mind-numbing and torturous abuse over several years at Ireland's famed Catholic institutions that cared for young women.

After enduring harrowing abuse by her father, O'Beirne claims that she was placed in the care of The Sisters of Our Lady of Charity at age 12 at a Magdalene laundry. She then chronicles atrocious and persistent abuse. With frightening detail, O'Beirne describes how the nuns at the laundries repeatedly brutalized her. One particular beating actually broke her pelvis, she writes. In addition, a priest raped her; at 13, she gave birth to a daughter, who died 10 years later. Abuse remained an ongoing hell at the laundries.

With the tsunami of clergy abuse stories from the United States still fresh in people's minds and scandals brewing in Ireland and England, O'Beirne harrowing tale took hold. Her chronicle enthralled readers. Her book reached number three on the UK's best-seller list, and it sold nearly 400,000 copies. Reviewers raved. The *Irish Independent* heralded the tome as "a devastating account of a childhood stolen by the twin evils of child abuse and an unholy church-state alliance."[2]

She magazine proclaimed, "Her story is so horrific, it's almost unbelievable."[3]

Well, as it turned out, the reason that *Kathy's Story* seemed "almost unbelievable" is simple: Ample evidence points to the conclusion that she made the whole thing up.

In September 2006, nearly a year after Kathy O'Beirne began her bestseller status, five of Kathy's brothers and sisters came forward publicly to address the media. They declared that their sister's book was a "hoax publication."[4] The siblings assured the public, "Our sister was not in a Magdalene laundry or Magdalene home."[5] With the exception of a six-week period at a home for troubled children, Kathy O'Beirne attended regular public schools.[6]

Indeed, The Sisters of Our Lady of Charity, who meticulously maintained their records, had no entry at all of the author ever being enrolled in a Magdalene laundry or home.

As for O'Beirne's claim that she gave birth at age 14, Mary O'Beirne, one of the author's younger sisters, said, "Until this book came out, she never once mentioned it."[7]

"There was never any mention of it in our household as we were growing up," the sister added. "There is no birth or death certificate. There is no child."[8]

Indeed, Kathy O'Beirne has never provided any documentation that she has ever given birth to anyone.

Priests never raped O'Beirne. A priest did not impregnate her.

"Our sister has a self-admitted psychiatric and criminal history, and her perception of reality has always been flawed," continued Mary. "We can understand that many people will now feel hurt and conned. Kathy is lying about all this, just like she has lied about things all her life. She is very convincing, though, and that is what makes her so dangerous."[9]

"Kathy has no credibility," Eamonn O'Beirne, one of Kathy's brothers, has said.[10]

Indeed, O'Beirne's co-author, a man by the name of Michael Sheridan, later admitted that the book's claims were unsupported.

"I'll tell you the evidence we have," said Sheridan. "There are no documents. Those documents are either falsified or destroyed. There is no evidence or records of Kathy in the two Magdalen laundries. There never was."[11]

Veteran writer Hermann Kelly exhaustively investigated O'Beirne's claims, and the evidence that he uncovered was astounding. Tearing the cover off O'Beirne's narrative, Mr. Kelly revealed that the woman's tale had all the hallmarks of fraud. Kelly's finds were so extensive that he catalogued them into an astonishing book, *Kathy's Real Story* (Ireland: Prefect Press, 2007).[12]

Especially upsetting to the O'Beirne siblings was Kathy's claim that their father was an abusive and terrifying man. In her book, Kathy writes of hideous torture by an angry, drunken thug.

In fact, the other O'Beirne children portray their father in the opposite manner, as a warm and supportive caregiver.

"My father never once lifted his hand to us. Never," Mary O'Beirne has said. "It was a normal, happy childhood. He was a very proud, good man, and it breaks my heart to see the terrible lies Kathy has written about him."[13]

"The anger and frustration we feel at seeing our father branded worldwide as a horrific abuser is indescribable," added Mary. "The allegations are untrue. We can't go on living like this. We can't eat. We can't sleep."[14]

The O'Beirne siblings were also upset at Kathy's publisher for failing to detect their sister's fraud. Mainstream Publishing, they argued, should have carried out the "necessary rigorous checks" before releasing such a book.

"If they had," the family said in a statement, "this book would never have been published."[15]

Yet, most amazingly, Kathy O'Beirne's venture continued to advance.

Even after the author's credibility was completely shattered, another book publisher actually announced that it had won a bid to put forth a *sequel* to O'Beirne's "story." Promotional materials said that the book would chronicle Kathy's "anorexia, suicide attempts and the story of hundreds of children she rescued and fostered."[16]

Upon hearing the news of a possible sequel, members of Kathy's family were understandably bewildered.

Kathy's brother reiterated her sister's history of mental instability. He exclaimed, "Who on earth would allow her to foster a child? I would call on the publishers to speak to Kathy's family before going ahead.

"Last time her target was the Church, and the book came out at a time of revelations about nuns and priests," Eamonn O'Beirne said. "When I saw her complaining about the health service in [a newspaper], I thought, here we go again. This time it will be the hospitals, doctors and nurses."[17]

After efforts by Kathy's brother and author Hermann Kelly to alert the publisher of O'Beirne's fraudulent claims, the publisher quietly announced in 2009, the year that it originally planned to release the sequel, that it was dropping the project because it had "failed to resolve legal issues"[18] with the author.

And if this tale could not get any more bizarre, *Kathy's Story* still continues to garner respectable sales in England and Ireland. Even years after being debunked, the book still receives glowing five-star reviews on Amazon.com's UK site.[19]

CATHOLIC PRIESTS FALSELY ACCUSED

NOTES AND REFERENCES

1 The book has also been published under the title, *Don't Ever Tell: A True Tale of a Childhood Destroyed by Neglect and Fear* (Mainstream Publishing, 2005/2006). (The spelling of the laundries have appeared historically as both "Magdalene" and "Magdalen.")

2 This quote is on the cover of the paperback of *Kathy's Story*.

3 This quote is on the cover of the paperback of *Don't Ever Tell*.

4 Natalie Clarke, "Author of child abuse memoir accused of fabricating her past," *Daily Mail* (U.K.), September 22, 2006.

5 Owen Bowcott, "Author's family deny tales of sex abuse," *The Guardian* (U.K.), September 19, 2006.

6 Hermann Kelly, "Lies of Little Miss Misery – memoir of abused girl is a fake, says new investigation," *Daily Mail*, (UK), October 31, 2007.

7 Clarke, September 22, 2006.

8 Ibid.

9 Esther Addley, "Author accused of literary fraud says: 'I am not a liar. And I am not running any more'," *The Guardian* (U.K.), September 22, 2006.

10 Colin Coyle, "Sequel to Kathy's Story sparks new furore," *The Sunday Times* (U.K.), October 26, 2008.

11 Hermann Kelly, "Kathy's co-writer admits a lack of facts," *The Sunday Times* (U.K.), September 24, 2006.

[12] Hermann Kelly, *Kathy's Real Story* (Ireland: Prefect Press). 2007.

[13] Clarke, September 22, 2006.

[14] Tim Cornwell, "Scots publisher linked to 'second made-up book' as author accused," *The Scotsman* (U.K.), September 20, 2006.

[15] David Sharrock, "Family point to 'glaring flaws' in abuse memoir," *The Sunday Times* (U.K.), September 20, 2006.

[16] Colin Coyle, "Publisher dumps sequel to Magdalene story," *The Sunday Times* (U.K.), July 26, 2009. The book was to be called *Always Dancing*.

[17] Colin Coyle, October 26, 2008.

[18] Colin Coyle, July 26, 2009.

[19] The Amazon UK listing with reviews is at http://www.amazon.co.uk/Kathys-Story-Childhood-Magdalen-Laundries/dp/1840189681

CATHOLIC PRIESTS FALSELY ACCUSED

19

Protecting Children

The Catholic Church's contributions to serving the poor, defending human rights, delivering healthcare, and providing education are unparalleled in history.

Yet one would never know this from the media. If one were to believe what television, newspapers, and the Internet constantly blare, the Church is an ancient cabal that callously harbors and fosters pedophiles. If one were to follow just the coverage of the *New York Times* (or the *Boston Globe*, actually), one could conclude that perverted Catholic priests are lurking everywhere with the sole purpose of raping every little boy they can get their hands on.

Meanwhile, research reveals sobering truths. Contemporaneous accusations against Catholic priests are quite rare. If one picks up a newspaper and reads an accusation of abuse against a Catholic priest, the allegation is almost *always* from decades earlier.

How many new accusations of abuse against a Catholic priest actually involve a person under the age of 18 at the time of the allegation? The Center for Applied Research in the Apostolate (CARA), the independent research organization out of Georgetown University, has been continuing to carefully track abuse data regarding United States Catholic clergy.

According to CARA, here are the numbers of abuse cases involving a *current minor* that were reported separately each year from 2005 to 2010:

Year	Number of allegations involving a current minor
2010	7
2009	6
2008	10
2007	4
2006	14
2005	9

Any number greater than zero is too many. However, the above numbers are indicative of an organization that has worked to rectify a serious problem.[1]

Contrast the numbers above with the fact that, according to the 2004 study by the John Jay College of Criminal Justice, 10,667 individuals made abuse allegations against 4,392 priests between 1950 and 2002. In addition, these numbers can be compared with the astronomical cases of abuse currently happening in our public schools (see previous chapter).

Indeed, the Church has experienced dark days as a result of criminal priests wreaking awful harm on innocent youth.

Yet the truth is that no other organization has worked more tirelessly in recent years to transform itself with the goal of protecting children. The major media will not report it, but the result is that the Catholic Church may be the safest environment for youth today.

Consider that in the United States, the Church:

- has trained over 6 million children in providing them skills to protect them from abuse (through specially designed programs created by prominent child-safety experts);
- has trained over 2 million adults, including over 99 percent of all priests, in recognizing signs of abuse;
- has conducted over 2 million background checks, including those in the intensified screening process for aspiring seminarians and priests;
- has installed reviews boards in nearly all dioceses, with the purpose of the boards being to thoroughly review all credible allegations of abuse; and
- has installed "Victim Assistance Coordinators" in every diocese, "assuring victims that they will be heard."[2],[3]

CATHOLIC PRIESTS FALSELY ACCUSED

The bishops implemented these measures with the goal of safety, despite the fact that there has never been any evidence that Catholic priests have offended more than those of any other denomination.[4]

And while the media and groups such as SNAP continue to portray the Church as a cold-hearted mob that turns its backs on abuse victims, the Church has paid out in the last several years:

- over $2 billion in legal settlements to those claiming abuse by priests (And as we've seen in this book, nearly *all* of these settlements were paid without any formal trial. In many cases, the priest was found to be innocent after the accuser had received a sizable settlement.); and
- nearly $70 million in therapy to victims.

And it must be repeated: While there has never been any evidence that Catholic clergy have abused minors more than those of other denominations; while nearly all Catholic clergy abuse occurred decades ago; while rampant abuses and cover-ups continue to happen today in our nation's public schools, no other organization has worked harder to safeguard children in its care than the Catholic Church.

NOTES AND REFERENCES

[1] My previous book, *Double Standard*, elaborated on this issue.

[2] Center for Applied Research in the Apostolate, "2009 Survey of Allegations and Costs: A Summary Report for the Secretariat of Child and Youth Protection, United States Conference of Catholic Bishops."

[3] United States Conference of Catholic Bishops (USCCB), "Charter for the Protection of Children and Young People: Essential Norms: Statement of Episcopal Commitment," Revised June 2005.

[4] I covered this issue in my previous book, *Double Standard*. For one source, however, see, "Mean Men," *Newsweek*, April 7, 2010.

20

Guilty or Falsely Accused?
The disputed case of
Fr. Gordon MacRae,
Diocese of Manchester, NH

The case of Father Gordon J. MacRae – from the
Diocese of Manchester, New Hampshire – falls into a
category all its own.

No single case in the Catholic Church abuse narrative has been more feverishly debated. The case has
bitterly polarized observers for several years. There are
those who maintain the priest's guilt and those who
forcefully assert his innocence.

Since 1994, Fr. MacRae has been incarcerated in
the New Hampshire State Prison for Men. On September 23, 1994, a jury convicted the priest of repeatedly
molesting a teenage boy during counseling sessions and

elsewhere. A judge later sentenced the cleric to 67 years in prison.

"Should the Case Against Father Gordon MacRae Be Reviewed?" That is the title to a compelling investigative article on the astonishing web site, TheseStoneWalls.com.

Fr. Gordon vehemently asserts his innocence and claims that he is falsely accused. With the help of outside supporters, an old typewriter, and the use of traditional postal mail, Fr. MacRae authors TheseStoneWalls.com from his small prison cell.

Fr. MacRae utilizes TheseStoneWalls.com not just as a forum to assert his innocence. Fr. Gordon also offers thoughtful spiritual and theological commentary. TheseStoneWalls.com is truly a compelling venue on the Internet.

What are the facts in this controversial case? Those who believe that Fr. Gordon's guilt is demonstrable gesture to reams of court documents and articles available at an anti-Church watchdog site.[1]

However, as with so many other cases, there is an alarming opposite side to Fr. MacRae's narrative that has not been widely told.

The criminal conviction of Fr. Gordon in 1994, which would catapult him to his sentence of 67 years in prison, rested on the uncorroborated testimony of one individual. The man's name is Thomas Grover. Amazingly, two of Thomas' brothers and two other men — known to the Grover boys — also accused Fr. Gordon of molesting them. Yet only the claims of Thomas Grover would be the subject of an actual criminal trial.

It is certainly a matter of debate whether the justice system yielded a fair trial for Fr. Gordon.

Although the accuser Grover had a lengthy juvenile criminal history of "theft, assault, forgery and drug offenses," the presiding judge, the Hon. Arthur D. Brennan, did not allow the priest's defense to present this as evidence.[2] Had the judge allowed this important information, the jury may have examined Grover's claims a bit more critically.

Indeed, Thomas Grover's accusations were quite tenable.

According to the court testimony of Grover, Fr. Gordon repeatedly sexually assaulted him about a decade earlier during four different counseling sessions in 1983, when he was fifteen years old.

Asked at trial why he would repeatedly return week after week to counseling sessions at which he had been previously attacked, Grover testified that he had "repressed" the memory of the experience after each assault. He claimed that he had an "out-of-body experience" which resulted in him completely forgetting the fact that he had been victimized during the previous visit.[3]

In addition, according to trial testimony, when Grover attended a drug treatment center in 1987, he told a counselor that his father had abused him. Grover did not cite the priest as an abuser. In fact, the accuser identified the priest by name to his counselor in only one instance. Grover wrote Fr. MacRae's name on his discharge contract indicating that the priest would be his sponsor in sobriety.[4]

In a previous deposition, Grover made more bizarre claims about Fr. Gordon, one of which was that the priest had chased him with a car.

"And he had a gun," the accuser added, "and he was threatening me and telling me over and over that he would hurt me, kill me, if I tried to tell anybody, that no one would believe me. He chased me through the cemetery and tried to corner me."[5]

However, at Fr. MacRae's trial, the prosecution did not call a single witness to corroborate the public spectacle of *a priest with a gun in a car chasing a boy through a cemetery.*

As the trial progressed, even the prosecution could see that Thomas Grover had serious credibility problems. In the middle of the trial, after Grover's flimsy appearance, the prosecution offered Fr. Gordon a plea bargain in which the priest would agree to serve only two years in jail in exchange for an admission of guilt.

It was not the first time the prosecution extended such a generous deal. On *two* other occasions before the court case – six months before trial and again a week before trial – the state offered plea deals to Fr. Gordon, both of which would ask that he serve no longer than three years in prison. The prosecution would have loved to have seen the priest take the offers.

But Fr. Gordon was adamant. He would not plead guilty to charges that he maintained were false. "I am not going to say I am guilty of crimes I never committed so that the Grovers and other extortionists can walk away with hundreds of thousands of dollars for their lies," the priest asserted.[6]

The trial progressed, and although Thomas Grover's testimony may have seemed hard to believe on the surface, the accuser was effectively theatrical during his appearance. He railed against the priest for "forcing" him to withstand the agony of a trial.[7]

In addition, during Grover's testimony, the accuser's therapist – retained by the man's contingency lawyer – reportedly coached her former patient while sitting in open view inside the courtroom.

Apparently directed by the therapist, Grover became emotional at strategic moments during his testimony. Courtroom witnesses have reported that when Grover was confronted with difficult questions, the therapist would gesture to her patient that he should cry. Grover would then become emotional and dramatic, often leading the judge to call a recess.[8]

Meanwhile, Judge Brennan purposefully ordered the jury to "disregard inconsistencies in Mr. Grover's testimony."[9]

To the shock of Fr. Gordon, the jury returned with a guilty verdict in less than 90 minutes.[10]

At Fr. Gordon's sentencing, the prosecution efficiently utilized accusations of abuse charges by other men. Stomach-turning stories of child pornography also impacted the jury.

An angry Judge Brennan railed against the convicted priest. He berated the cleric for his "lack of remorse" over his crimes. (Lost on the judge was the fact that the priest forcefully maintained his innocence and had rejected *three* different plea offers.)

Building upon his rage, the judge added, "The evidence of your possession of child pornography is clear and convincing."

There was one problem, however. "There was never any evidence of child pornography," the lead detective on the case later admitted.[11]

Under New Hampshire prison guidelines, Fr. Gordon will never be eligible for parole unless he admits guilt.

As with the case of Msgr. McCarthy (Chapter 6), Father Gordon's narrative highlights the zeal with which some detectives will seek a prosecution, despite the claims presented to them.

The criminal case against Fr. Gordon actually began when one of Thomas Grover's *brothers*, Jonathan, approach Keene, New Hampshire, Detective James McLaughlin with the claim that Fr. Gordon had abused him years earlier. However, Jonathan did not just accuse Fr. Gordon of abuse; he accused a second priest as well – Fr. Stephen Scruton.[12]

However, as Detective McLaughlin further examined Jonathan's claims, he realized that Fr. Scruton did not even serve at the parish of the alleged abuse until years after Jonathan claimed that the acts took place.

With this startling discovery of fact, many detectives would have concluded that Jonathan was not being truthful. There would even be more reason to doubt

Jonathan when two of his brothers came forward to claim similar abuse by the two priests.

But rather than dropping the investigation altogether and issuing charges against Jonathan for filing a false report, McLaughlin continued his crusade by simply *scrubbing the existence of Fr. Scruton* from future investigations altogether.[13]

In the course of trying to nab Fr. MacRae, McLaughlin initiated a couple of attempted "stings" to get the priest to admit to the alleged abuse. One was a letter claiming to be from Jonathan Grover that "recalled" several sexual escapades and declared that the "sex between us was very special." Fr. Gordon replied to the letter by saying that the letter writer must be an imposter, because no such acts ever took place.[14]

McLaughlin also attempted a number of secretly recorded phone calls to try to bust the priest, but none of them yielded anything incriminating. The calls were an utter failure, by all investigative measures.

Fr. Gordon would have been out of prison long ago if he had accepted the plea deals and admitted guilt. Instead, in staunchly maintaining his innocence, he will likely live in a prison cell for the remainder of his life.

In recent years, even more evidence has surfaced to support the claim that Fr. Gordon was falsely accused. One of the priest's accusers (not Thomas Grover) has reportedly recanted his claims. In early 2011, a document surfaced in which the accuser plainly acknowledges that fraud was committed against Fr.

Gordon and the Catholic Church. According to a New York investigative writer, the document says:

> "I was aware at the time of the [pending 1994] trial, knowing full well that it was all bogus and having heard of the lawsuits and money involved, and also the reputations of those making accusations ... whom I went to school with.
> It seemed as though it would be easy money if I would also accuse Gordon of some wrongdoing. ... I believed easy money would come from lawsuits against MacRae. I was at the time using drugs and could have been influenced to say anything they wanted for money."[15]

So despite the tempting opportunity of a high-stakes payout, the man refused to go along with what he saw was a gross money-grubbing scam.

In 2005, Pulitzer Prize-winning writer Dorothy Rabinowitz profiled the case of Fr. Gordon for a pair of eye-opening articles for the *Wall Street Journal*. After months of studying court documents and combing through testimonies, Rabinowitz concluded that Fr. MacRae was clearly a victim of fraud and was wrongly convicted.[16]

Sadly, under intense public pressure from events of the past decade, Church officials have essentially abandoned Fr. Gordon. Despite the fact that evidence possibly indicating innocence continues to surface, Church officials have kept their distance from the incarcerated cleric. While Church officials have *publicly* supported the prosecution of Fr. Gordon, there are reports that *privately* they admit that the cleric may have been falsely accused.

For example, in 2011, two signed statements surfaced which claim that Bishop John McCormack, the longtime head of the Diocese of Manchester, has privately stated that he believes Fr. Gordon is innocent.

One such statement comes from a man who once worked at a television station that was to profile Fr. Gordon's case. It quotes Bishop McCormack as saying to the man, "Understand, none of this is to leave this office. I believe Father MacRae is not guilty and his accusers likely lied."

"There's nothing I can do to change the verdict," Bishop McCormack also said, according to the statement.[17]

The man submitted his statement about Bishop McCormack's remarks because he believed there was a glaring injustice in the inconsistency between the prelate's public actions and his private statements.

"Should the Case Against Father Gordon MacRae Be Reviewed?" Considering the totality of the evidence, especially that which has surfaced in recent years, the answer is, "Yes."

Justice demands it.

In addition, recent developments and emerging information will likely result in appeals of Fr. MacRae's case. Stay tuned.

NOTES AND REFERENCES

[1] www.BishopAccountability.org

[2] Dorothy Rabinowitz, "A Priest's Story," *Wall Street Journal,* April 28, 2005. P. A18.

[3] Ryan A. MacDonald, "Trial by Therapists," TheseStone-Walls.com, August 2, 2011.

[4] Ryan A. MacDonald, "Truth in Justice: Was the Wrong Catholic Priest Sent to Prison?" TheseStoneWalls.com, April 6, 2011.

[5] Rabinowitz.

[6] Ibid.

[7] Ibid.

[8] MacDonald, August 2, 2011.

[9] Rabinowitz.

[10] Ibid.

[11] Ibid.

[12] MacDonald, April 6, 2011.

[13] Ibid.

[14] Rabinowitz.

[15] Ryan A. MacDonald, "Should the Case Against Father Gordon MacRae Be Reviewed?" TheseStoneWalls.com, April 5, 2010.

[16] Two parts: Dorothy Rabinowitz, "A Priest's Story," *Wall Street Journal*, April 27 and 28, 2005.

[17] The author has viewed this statement.

CATHOLIC PRIESTS FALSELY ACCUSED

21

Ahead

In 1983, astonishing accusations of satanic child sexual abuse were made against operators and employees of the Virginia McMartin Preschool in Manhattan Beach, California.

As the story swelled, news reports blared shocking tales of "children being raped and sodomized, of dead rabbits, mutilated corpses and a horse killing, and of blood drinking, satanic rituals and the sacrifice of a live baby in a church."[1]

A trial began in 1984, and prosecutors charged seven McMartin employees with 321 counts of child abuse. At one point, the case employed "three DAs fulltime, fourteen investigators from the DA's office, twenty-two task force officers, two fulltime social workers, twenty part-time social workers, a fulltime detective and four part-time detectives. They had searched twenty-one residences, seven businesses, three churches, two airports, thirty-seven cars, and a farm."[2]

A voracious media could not get enough of the story. It all but convicted the accused individuals. A 1984 television report shocked viewers with the claim that 60 children "have now each told authorities that he or she had been keeping a grotesque secret of being sexually abused and made to appear in pornographic films while in the preschool's care – and of having been forced to witness the mutilation and killing of animals to scare the kids into staying silent."[3]

A deputy district attorney added that law enforcement had uncovered "millions of child pornography photographs and films" from the McMartins, as the main purpose of the abuse was the production of child pornography.[4]

When the narrative ended in 1990, it was California's most expensive and longest-running trial.

Yet it turned out the actual number of children that the McMartins had abused was *zero*. And not a single frame or image of child pornography was ever presented.[5]

The entire case began with flimsy accusations from a mentally ill woman, whose son attended the daycare. Her allegations were the delusions of a paranoid schizophrenic, it was later learned, and the jury never heard this.[6] Ambitious prosecutors, unscrupulous child therapists, and an uncritical media enabled the case to snowball out of control.

The false accusations, the media circus, and the years-long trial thrashed the lives of scores of innocent families.[7]

It would be convenient to think that all of the reports of criminal child abuse by Catholic priests were just wild concoctions – like the McMartin episode. Unfortunately, this is far from the case. However, the McMartin narrative delivers valuable lessons. Consumers must be cautious of the media, especially with regards to reports on the emotional topic of child abuse.

Indeed, these have been dark days for the Catholic Church. The sins of criminal priests have vandalized the reputation of the Church and begat indescribable damage upon innocent minors. These atrocities must never be dismissed, and victims cannot be forgotten.

There is little doubt that – in one sense – the tsunami of media coverage in the last two decades has actually been a benefit to the Church. News coverage has shone a light on the darkness and enabled the Church to rid itself of the "filth" of child abuse. (And "filth" is the word with which Pope Benedict has described child abuse.)

But what about our priests? Even after being exonerated, innocent men find that the stigma of an accusation always remains with them. Even the reputations of defenseless, deceased priests have been tarnished.

A longtime friend of an accused priest told him after he was exonerated, "No matter what happens to you in the future, even though you were cleared, no

matter where you go, there will be always be people who
will point you out and say, 'That's the priest.' And they
will say what they want to say about you. That's going
to be part of your history now."

Sadly, an accusation will almost always become
part of a man's priestly identity over which he has little
control.

What can lay Catholics do?
Here are some ideas:

1. Catholics can pray for priests. Here is one excellent
prayer:

Dear Lord,
I pray for Your faithful and fervent priests,
the priests who are falling away from the Host,
the true and living God,
the priests who labor at home and in distant
mission fields,
the tempted and disobedient priests, the lonely
and desolate priests,
the young and old priests, the sick and dying
priests and
the souls of Your priests in Purgatory.
But especially for the priests who are dearest to
me;
the priest who baptized me; the priests who have
absolved me of my sins;
the priests at whose Mass I have assisted and
have given me Your Body and Blood in

Holy Communion;
the priests who have taught and instructed me
and to whom I am indebted in any way.
Please keep them close to Your Heart, for they
are in Your Heart,
and bless them abundantly in time
and in eternity.
Amen [8]

2. Catholics can pray for the Church.

In an excellent February 2011 article, Catholic evangelist Gary Zimak reminds the faithful of an important truth. As a devotee of evil, Satan takes great joy when the Church is attacked and damaged. While we must continue to pray and demand justice and compassion for real victims of clergy abuse, we must not let anger play into the hands of Old Scratch. Catholics do this by speaking irresponsibly about priests and recklessly condemning the Church. Zimak explains:

> "When we condemn 'The Church,' we fail to recognize that there is a difference between 'The Church' and her individual members. When one of her members (including members of the Church hierarchy) sins, it is not 'The Church' who sins, but the individuals!"[9]

As the Church continues to combat abuse and help victims, there is an extraordinary opportunity to affirm the "foundation and pillar of truth" (1 Tim. 3:15).

CATHOLIC PRIESTS FALSELY ACCUSED

By praying for the Church, Catholics can deflect Satan's ongoing attempt to distract them from this mission.[10]

Oremus.

NOTES AND REFERENCES

[1] Robert Reinhold, "The Longest Trial – A Post-Mortem," *New York Times*, January 24, 1990.

[2] Katherine Ramsland, Ph.D., "The McMartin Nightmare and the Hysteria Puppeteers," http://www.trutv.com/library/crime/criminal_mind/psychology /mcmartin_daycare/1.html

[3] Reinhold.

[4] David Shaw, "Where Was Skepticism in Media?: Pack journalism and hysteria marked early coverage of the McMartin case," *Los Angeles Times*, January 19, 1990. Highly recommended.

[5] Ibid.

[6] See Ramsland. Also, Douglas O. Linder, J.D., "The McMartin Preschool Abuse Trial: A Commentary," University of Missouri – Kansas City, 2003. http://law2.umkc.edu/faculty/projects/ftrials/mcmartin/mcmar tinaccount.html

[7] One may also want to look up the astonishing case of Gerald Amirault and "Fells Acre Day Dare" in Massachusetts. Mr. Amirault served 18 years in jail for crimes that no clear-thinking person would think actually occurred. For one, see

Dorothy Rabinowitz, *No Crueler Tyrannies* (New York: Free Press), 2003.

[8] I believe the original source of this prayer is "Prayer for Priests," by Oblates of the Virgin Mary, www.omvusa.org

[9] Gary Zimak, "Satan's Attack on the Church – What You Can Do!" CatholicLane.com, February 22, 2011. http://catholiclane.com/satan%E2%80%99s-attack-on-the-church-%E2%80%93-what-you-can-do/

[10] Ibid.

CATHOLIC PRIESTS FALSELY ACCUSED

Index

Index

Recommended by Dave Pierre

Catholicism / Catholic Living

o *The Catechism of the Catholic Church* (New York: Doubleday, 1994) ... What the Church *really* teaches ... from the Church itself!

o *Ignatius Catholic Study Bible New Testament: RSV Second Catholic Edition* (Ignatius Press, 2010) ... Dr. Scott Hahn and Curtis Mitch have created a marvelous study Bible.

o Anything by Peter Kreeft ... Author of over 40 books. A huge influence. *The Handbook of Christian Apologetics, Socrates Versus Marx, How to Win the Culture War, The Journey* ... many more.

o Matt Swaim, *Prayer in the Digital Age* (Ligouri Publications, 2011). The longer I am on this computer typing, the more I am on the Internet and checking my e-mail for umpteenth time of the day, the more I realize I need to go back to this book. A terrific read. And very important.

Recommended by the Author

o Gus Lloyd, *A Minute in the Church*, (2010). One-minute Catholic apologetics! This handy, easy-to-read booklet is extremely useful and helpful. A must-have.

o The Linacre Institute, *After Asceticism: Sex, Prayer and Deviant Priests* (AuthorHouse, 2006). "The first study of its find, [this book] shows how the infiltration of therapeutic psychology on the training and lifestyles of clergy spawned a cavalier attitude in many priests and bishops about sex and prayer, causing the collapse of ascetical discipline with its devastating effects in the sex abuse crisis." Excellent.

o Gary Zimak, "Satan's Attack on the Church – What You Can Do!" February 22, 2011, www.catholiclane.com

Uncovering fraud

o Dorothy Rabinowitz, *No Crueler Tyrannies: Accusation, False Witness, and Other Terrors of Our Times* (Free Press, 2004). The case of Gerald Amirault should shock every honest American.

o Hermann Kelly, *Kathy's Real Story: A Culture of False Allegations Exposed* (Dublin: Prefect Press, 2007). Highly recommended.

CATHOLIC PRIESTS FALSELY ACCUSED

o Monsignor William McCarthy, *The Conspiracy: An Innocent Priest* (iUniverse, 2010). An astonishing, extensive, first-person account by a falsely accused priest.

o Brendan O'Neill, "How the New Atheists are abusing the truth," spiked-online.com, September 2010.

Newspapers/Magazines

o *National Catholic Register*

o *New Oxford Review*

o *This Rock* ... Catholic apologetics and evangelization

Internet

o www.NCRegister.com ... Tim Drake, Jimmy Akin, Mark Shea, and much more. Essential!

o ThePulp.it ... A huge service. Tito Edwards combs through the best of the Catholic blogosphere, so we don't have to. On most days there are morning *and* afternoon listings.

o www.CatholicVote.org ... Great Catholic voices, such as American Papist, Thomas Peters.

Recommended by the Author

- www.CatholicLeague.org ... The Catholic League for Religious and Civil Rights: The organization combating anti-Catholicism in the U.S.

- www.CatholicCulture.org ... Smart, informative, Phil Lawler.

- www.OpusBono.org ... Opus Bono Sacerdotii ("Work for the Good of the Priesthood")

- www.Catholic.com ... Catholic Answers: A fantastic resource for authentic Catholic information.

- www.NewsBusters.org ... Exposing liberal media bias. A forum of the Media Research Center. I'm a contributing writer.

- www.TheMediaReport.com ... My web site! "Examining anti-Catholicism and bias in the media."

Television and radio

- *EWTN* ... Television and radio. My Sirius satellite radio has been a gift with EWTN radio. I especially appreciate "The Son Rise Morning Show," hosted by Brian Patrick, with Matt Swaim and Anna Mitchell; "Catholic Connection" with Teresa Tomeo; "Women of Grace" with Johnnette Benkovic; and "Kresta in the Afternoon" (with Al Kresta).

o *The Catholic Channel* ... Also on my Sirius satellite radio. I am very grateful to have benefited much from "Seize the Day with Gus Lloyd" and "The Catholics Next Door" with Greg and Jennifer Willits.

o *Relevant Radio* ... Drew Mariani does a terrific afternoon show.

o CatholicTV ... Fr. Robert Reed.

Also by Dave Pierre:
Double Standard: Abuse Scandals and the Attack on the Catholic Church

Double Standard: Abuse Scandals and the Attack on the Catholic Church is fast-paced, informative, startling, unapologetic, and impeccably researched.

"*Double Standard: Abuse Scandals and the Attack on the Catholic Church* is **essential reading** for anyone who wants to hear the other side of the clergy sexual abuse scandal ... Even for someone who has read about this subject for years, it was **eye-opening** to me ... If someone attacks you or slanders the Church over the sexual abuse scandal, challenge them to read this book and continue saying such things." – **Thomas Peters, American Papist, CatholicVote.org**

"**For anyone who wants to defend the Church against unfair attacks** – or simply to separate the unfair attacks from those that are on target – this book is a **useful resource** ... His book makes a clear and documented case that the media coverage of the crisis has distorted public perceptions." – **Phil Lawler, CatholicCulture.org**

"The book is **incredibly focused** ... His message is simple: There is a double standard involved in the prosecution of abuse cases. There is a one-sided bias that assumes any priest who has been accused is 'guilty until proven guiltier'." – **The American Society for the Defense of Tradition, Family and Property**

Yes, Catholic priests terribly abused minors, and bishops failed to stop the unspeakable harm. That is an undeniable truth. Nothing justifies such an evil. The damage to victims is immeasurable.

However, major media outlets are unfairly attacking the Catholic Church, and this compelling book has the shocking evidence to prove it.

Double Standard addresses numerous topics, including:
... appalling cases of abuse and cover-ups happening today – but they're not happening in the Catholic Church;
... proof that Catholic clergy do not offend more than teachers or those of other religious denominations;
... data that shows that the Catholic clergy scandal is not about "pedophilia";
... affirmation that the Catholic Church may be the safest environment for children today;
... research that uncovers the shady relationships between SNAP (Survivors Network of Those Abused by Priests), lawyers, and the media;
... convincing documentation that the national spokesperson of SNAP once failed to report suspected child abuse himself – while he was SNAP's spokesperson;
... the astonishing connection between SNAP and the radical community group ACORN;
... evidence of how the Hollywood "documentary" *Deliver Us From Evil* deceived moviegoers;
plus much more ...

Double Standard covers topics that the major media won't. There is no other book about the Catholic Church abuse narrative like this one.

Made in the USA
Charleston, SC
25 January 2012